BOB DYLAN IN THE ATTIC

A Volume in the Series
AMERICAN POPULAR MUSIC
Edited by
Jeffrey Melnick

BOB DYLAN IN THE ATTIC

THE ARTIST AS HISTORIAN

FREDDY CRISTÓBAL DOMÍNGUEZ

University of Massachusetts Press
Amherst and Boston

ISBN 978-1-62534-681-0 (paper); 682-7 (hardcover)
Designed by Sally Nichols
Set in Monotype Baskerville Pro
Printed and bound by Books International, Inc.
Cover design by Derek Thornton, Notch Design
Cover photo by Sharon Mollerus, detail of mural *The Times They Are
A-changin'*, by Eduardo Kobra, 2017. CC.02.

Library of Congress Cataloging-in-Publication Data

Names: Domínguez, Freddy Cristóbal, 1982–author.
Title: Bob Dylan in the attic : the artist as historian / Freddy Cristóbal
Domínguez.
Description: Amherst : University of Massachusetts Press, 2022. | Series:
American popular music | Includes bibliographical references and index.
Identifiers: LCCN 2022022503 (print) | LCCN 2022022504 (ebook) | ISBN
9781625346810 (paperback) | ISBN 9781625346827 (hardcover) | ISBN
9781613769614 (ebook) | ISBN 9781613769621 (ebook)
Subjects: LCSH: Dylan, Bob, 1941—Criticism and interpretation. | Popular
music—History and criticism. | Music and history.
Classification: LCC ML420.D98 D65 2022 (print) | LCC ML420.D98 (ebook) |
DDC 782.42164092—dc23/eng/20220511
LC record available at https://lccn.loc.gov/2022022503
LC ebook record available at https://lccn.loc.gov/2022022504

British Library Cataloguing-in-Publication Data
A catalog record for this book is available from the British Library.

Portions of chapter 1 were previously published as "Into the Library, Into the
Past: Bob Dylan's Sense of History," in *New Approaches to Bob Dylan*, ed.
Anne-Marie Mai (Odense: University Press of Southern Denmark, 2020), 233–46.

FOR MARY

CONTENTS

PREFACE

I think authors writing about religious figures should state their confessional allegiances. Since Bob Dylan has attained spiritual status among some readers, fans, and followers, I should underline my noncultic relationship to him. Although I own all his records, a good number of bootlegs (official and unofficial), and have seen him whenever I've been close by—Nashville, London, Manhattan (twice), Brooklyn, Long Island, Tulsa, Rome, and Murray (Kentucky)—I can claim only minor-league status among his most impassioned fans. Consequently, this book is not written from a fan's perspective—it is not written admiringly or with "Dylanological" obsessiveness beyond the limits of what research and serious thought requires. I have not, will never, and have no interest in meeting Dylan, getting his autograph, or owning rare memorabilia linked to him. I write as an academic who believes that distance can be a virtue. I also write with full confidence that Dylan himself would think a lot of this is bullshit and with a mostly respectful belief that much of what Dylan says is bullshit, too. This book, as I will say again in a few pages, is only a vehicle for understanding things that are greater than himself, although I think Dylan—the performer—is undoubtedly great.

ACKNOWLEDGMENTS

I am proud of this book. I didn't write it for money or professional advancement but out of pure curiosity and love of the game. I've come to appreciate the beauty in that.

The desire to write these pages first stirred more than a decade ago while I was walking down Montague Street, but the notion didn't congeal until I wandered the streets of Odense. Attending a conference on Dylan at the University of Southern Denmark—"New Approaches to Bob Dylan"—revealed just how rich scholarship on Dylan is. I thought it would be great to be part of that crowd. My thanks to Dr. Anne-Marie Mai for convening the event and for the stimulation provided by all participants.

My deep thanks to Brian Halley and Jeff Melnick at the University of Massachusetts Press for taking a risk with this book and for their patience along the way.

There were times when I doubted that *Bob Dylan in the Attic* would ever be finished, or worse, when I was taking things too seriously and killing the fun. On more than one occasion Patrick Williams talked to me in Dylanese, which made me laugh. On a particularly desolate night, I got an e-mail from him in that strange language and it kept me going. The little things.

Writing a book is all-absorbing and difficult. It would be impossible without my family, all of whom couldn't care less about Dylan.

Thanks to my parents, as always, for their unflinching love and patience.

Thanks to Nana and Pa for their kindness and for watching the littles from time to time so I can recharge.

Thank you to Laura for her zaniness, Vivian for her sweetness, and Santi for being the feral gremlin that he is. Thank you to Niccolò for showing me how the light gets in.

It's hard to thank someone who means everything. But maybe I can start by recalling with gratitude a trip my wife, Mary, took with me to see Dylan in Murray, Kentucky. I remember she wore something white. Torrential rains fell and the backroads were flooding—we couldn't get back to Nashville that night and were forced to make do with questionable and overpriced quarters. What a luxury to share the same place and space, then and now. Since those days she has stood by me when the waters have risen and when I've seen the darkness. I dedicate this book to her knowing that the gesture is small compared to what she has given me.

I last saw Dylan with my (step)daughter, Rose. There was a French guy between us that did not want to move. She found the whole affair "interesting." I was grateful to her for humoring me. I am grateful that she has let me be part of her life and that I've gotten to see her become the awesome young woman that she is. When this book appears, she will have started—God willing—a beautiful new life full of adventure, discovery, revelation, and good books. Here's hoping, as Dylan did for his children, that you stay "forever young."

BOB DYLAN IN THE ATTIC

INTRODUCTION

OUT OF THE PAST

In a rare performance of curiosity, Bob Dylan listened to what Gregory Peck had to say. During the 1998 Kennedy Center Awards Gala, Dylan sat hunched forward, eyes at a squint, expectant. Maybe it was a guy thing. Bill Clinton beamed, while opera diva Jessye Norman sat solemnly and Hillary Clinton smirked between Bob and Bill. Whatever Dylan was thinking—and who will ever know for sure?—he probably felt satisfied. Apart from the praise, he likely enjoyed knowing that an important part of his act had succeeded: he had bent time.

Peck started with a story. Once, some time ago, he had seen Civil War veterans "kicking up dust" at a parade in California. They immediately came to mind when he first heard Dylan: "I thought of him as something of a Civil War type, a kind of nineteenth-century troubadour, a maverick American spirit. The reediness of his voice and the spareness of his words go straight to the heart of America."[1] Peck made an icon out of Dylan, a hallowed image, the essence of a nation, its embodiment and invoker. Dylan raises Civil War ghosts through his sepia-tinted performance style and in doing so says something fundamental about a country born of song and blood. In

Peck's telling, Dylan, by acts of performative magic, emerges spectrally from the past.

Recently, many have spoken about Dylan within the context of times and places more distant than nineteenth-century America. Paul Simon, for example, wanted to enlist Dylan for the title track of *So Beautiful or So What* (2015) because his tattered voice would provide an air of antiquity: "He would sound like a sage."[2] The aura of primordial wisdom comes from his voice's natural withering, but it's also a consequence of loftier perceptions and cultural needs. Dylan is a link to an old Western tradition, to the Canon many (academics) have tried to kill to no avail. T-Bone Burnett, recalling a trope that emerged at the start of Dylan's career, dubs him "the Homer of our time,"[3] while Bono calls him "our own Willy Shakespeare in a polka-dot shirt."[4]

Dylan has also put himself in fine, dead company. In his Nobel Banquet Speech (2017) he evoked The Bard, suggesting that in its mundanity his process is Shakespearean: "Like Shakespeare, I too am often occupied with the pursuit of my creative endeavors and dealing with all aspects of life's mundane matters. 'Who are the best musicians for these songs?' 'Am I recording in the right studio?' 'Is this song in the right key?' Some things never change, even in four hundred years."[5] Dylan's art goes back to Homer, too. In his Nobel Lecture (2017), he says his words are meant to be sung, not read, and in this way his poetry is like an ancient heroic ballad. He returns to immortal lines from *The Iliad*: "Sing in me, oh Muse, and through me tell the story."[6]

Dylan might belong on Mount Olympus, but he also places himself within earthier traditions. As he told a room full of journalists in Rome before the release of *"Love and Theft"* (2001), his music is based on "blues formats or twelve bar formats."[7] Dylan looks to greats like Robert Johnson and to the blues' mysterious, "exotic" roots, which he cryptically traces back to a blend of Arabic violins and Strauss waltzes.[8]

Dylan also places himself within a centuries-old "folk" tradition. Like the nineteenth-century folklorists who tried to trace American culture to its British origins, Dylan says his work goes back to Elizabethan England and its songs. He looks beyond Shakespeare to the margins of sixteenth-century society: "These songs of mine, I think of as mystery plays, the kind that Shakespeare saw when he was growing up. I think you could trace what I do back that far. They were on the fringes then, and I think they're on the fringes now. And they sound like they've been traveling on hard ground."[9] The Shakespearean link is not lost here, but Dylan knows that he and the playwright tap a deeper quarry.

The emphasis on old musical traditions betrays a special intimacy with them. Clinton Heylin, Dylan's most prolific and obsessive biographer, says that Dylan wants us to think he is "almost channeling" old-time singers. Dylan believes his connection to various musical pasts sets him apart from the present: "People who came after me, I don't really feel, were ever my peers or contemporaries, because they didn't really have any standing in traditional music." There were a lot of imitators, but they failed to go back to the sources, and so "those songs don't have any resonance."[10] He maintains, "Folk music is where it all starts and in many ways ends. If you don't have that foundation, or if you're not knowledgeable about it . . . and you don't feel historically tied to it, then what you're doing is not going to be as strong as it could be."[11] As novelist Jonathan Lethem sees it, "Dylan seems to feel he dwells in a body haunted like a house by his bardlike musical precursors."[12] Speaking about his own songs on *Modern Times* (2006), Dylan described how he "just let the lyrics go" and as he sang them "they seemed to have an ancient presence."[13]

The shadow of antiquity in his work and self-appraisal justifies what might, at first, seem like a silly question: Is Bob Dylan a historian? At least one professional historian thinks the question legitimate and the answer affirmative. In his groundbreaking *Bob Dylan in America*, Sean Wilentz follows Dylan's own words to describe how he "discovered the cuneiforms of his art in the microfilm room," how the lifeblood of his art emerged out of serious knowledge of primary sources, original documents from the nineteenth century.[14] While promoting the book, Wilentz went further in recruiting Dylan to

Clio's tribe. He claimed Dylan showed him "you can see the past in the present" and in that collapse Wilentz identified "the beginnings of historical consciousness."[15] The uncanny ability to fold time over itself resulted from a finely tuned "historical sensibility" that makes Dylan a de facto historian, if not one by profession or degree. Wilentz—a Princeton professor with considerable public reach—concludes that "he [Dylan] is a better historian than I am."[16]

Over fifty years earlier Dylan had been called a historian by a fellow musician. It was meant as an insult. Dave Van Ronk, a giant on the Village music scene and one of Dylan's mentors early on, had had enough of Dylan's "hillbilly" schtick and his imitation of Woody Guthrie (or maybe his imitation of Ramblin' Jack Elliott's imitation of Guthrie). During one outburst Van Ronk chastised Dylan and told him to stop rewriting songs from the thirties: "Do your own songs. Their songs are for the history books. You're just going to be a history book writer if you do those things. An anachronism."[17] These were fighting words that beautifully bring together intertwined elements of Dylan's historical persona: in "writing" a kind of history, Dylan embodies it, becoming, as Van Ronk suggested, a relic of a past not his own.

This book is not combative, so it does not start with Van Ronk but picks up where Wilentz left off. While *Dylan in America* places Dylan's oeuvre within rich historical contexts, Wilentz does not delve into the historicist aspects of his music. His book discusses what makes Dylan's work historically evocative, but it does not focus on Dylan's brand of history making. My excuse for this book is therefore to explore the unexplored. If plenty of ink has been spilled on how Dylan draws on musical and literary genres, there has been no deep discussion about Dylan's historical modalities, how he goes about constructing a sense of history, and how his work has been perceived through a historical lens.[18]

The question of whether Dylan is a historian, while central to this book, ended up being only a starting point. After some twists and turns, it has become a study about forms of historical representation. There are surely more obvious points of entry to such a vast topic, but over ten years ago, on a cold dark night, after watching Dylan's craggy, dust-ridden performance of "Maggie's Farm" on television, I started to think about studying it from an oblique angle. I have the heart of a "microhistorian" and so count myself among those who study the particular and even the exceptional to understand the generic and unexceptional: the exceptional tests the limits of normalcy *and* contains within it the coordinates of the normative. Thus, the goal here is not to claim that Dylan will give us insights into any one historical method but to suggest that by studying his formative historical experiences, how he himself has "done" history, and that which has been perceived as historical in his work, we can better understand the amplitude of modern historical culture. Because we are looking at history from a nontraditional point of view, I hope the results are disorienting but also informative of what history can look like.

This book is not based on a precise or strict theory of history. Indeed, the point here is to show how Dylan engages with the past and how he re-presents it, how he mediates historical materials into being for current consumption. By studying Dylan's engagement with the past, I want to show history in action devoid of preconceptions except the very basic notion that history (as an activity) can be simply (perhaps too simply) defined as the study of the past, and the historian as anyone who wants to *re-present* the past and does so *intentionally*. As we'll see, there is plenty of evidence that Dylan is interested in the past and that he actively wants to re-create it through music and other means.

The fact that Dylan is a musical performer matters. Unfortunately, even with the expansion of "recognized" historical forms—film, theater, photography, museum exhibits, novels, etcetera—music has not loomed large or often at all.[19] As a result, this book seeks inspiration from musicological studies, including work on "revivals" that are part and parcel of modern musical traditions, most notably in folk, but also in (once) "popular" forms such as doo-wop.[20] Studies on tribute bands, musicians on revival circuits, and folk performers show that much musical work depends on a credible archaeology of musical pasts, the findings of which are displayed performatively using techniques of imitation and reconstruction that we'd be hard-pressed not to call "historical." And yet, with notable exceptions, the idea of music (and musical performance) as history has not had much traction.[21] So, in his brilliant *Retromania*, Simon Reynolds has catalogued the many ways that pop music, and pop culture more generally, comes circling back to its past, but strangely does not see many practices of referencing, collecting, or reperforming as part of a properly historical enterprise.[22] Given this reticence, a case study on Dylan and history might suggest some ways that music making and history making can be mutually reinforcing.

Ultimately, this book stakes its value on the idea that taking all historical forms—including musical ones—seriously is worthwhile, because it gives us a deeper sense of, as George Lipsitz puts it, "the importance of historical thinking as an organic and necessary way of understanding human experience, a mode of organizing ideas and interpretations that is as indispensable in everyday life as it is in scholarly research."[23] From where I sit, as a history professor, I am happy to belong to a specific historical tradition and am happy to help spawn others (as a teacher and adviser) who do things pretty much as I have been taught to do them, but I can also recognize that I am sharing a space of historical reconstruction with many others who are not part of academe and who do not play by the same rules but still have a voice—almost always a voice much louder than mine—in representing the past. As Jill Lepore has described in her book about the modern Tea Party in American politics, stilted and plain wrong history, loudly proclaimed and in period garb, can leave a deep imprint.[24]

WARNING!

I hope my intentions are intelligible thus far, but a few caveats are worthwhile.

The following pages are *not* about Dylan as a historical figure or how he changed history. Here he emerges not as an innovator, avatar, or guiding light but as an artist very much of his cultural milieu, a traveler down a beaten path trying to make sense of the relationship between past and present using concepts and approaches that are sometimes quite old.

Here I take for granted, as so many others have shown, that Dylan pillages from the past. I am *not* interested in revealing thefts in themselves but in discussing how these activities fit within coordinates of history making.

This project is *not* primarily interested in deciphering the "meaning" of any song. Instead, when I deal with specific songs, their composition, and performance, I try to understand how they reveal something about Dylan's ideas about history and his techniques of historical re-creation.

Finally, readers will surely notice that scholarship on Dylan's work as historian has been produced by a relatively exclusive club of white men. I suspect this is symptomatic of some unhappy realities regarding the demographics of rock criticism and the academy. Maybe it also says something about who feels most implicated by his work. Fortunately, the trend in Dylan scholarship is toward the inclusion of a more diverse set of voices, and I hope that future work on Dylan and history will include that diversity.

THE PLAN

If you are still reading and willing to come along for the ride, here is how we'll go. Chapter 1 is a kaleidoscopic effort to understand the historical traditions that have influenced Dylan. The next two chapters discuss Dylan as history maker. In chapter 2, I explore various historical techniques that allow Dylan to create illusions of the past. Chapter 3 discusses Dylan's mythological approach to history and the mythological function of his historical work. Chapter 4 leaves Dylan himself behind to consider how others have interpreted his work historically. At this point we will have traveled from Dylan's brain to the brain of his listeners—we will have traveled a path from historical ideas, through practices, and ultimately to reception. Chapter 5 takes an off-ramp to think about Dylan's authorial persona and the reasons why he feels emboldened to, or capable of, doing the historical work this book describes.

ONE LAST THING

Researchers often succumb to their subjects. To an extent, I have too. Although this book, for better or worse, is (mostly) free of a habit among Dylanologists (big and small) to imitate Dylan's wordsmithery or glibly insert Dylan's lyrics into their prose, there is something sub-Dylanesque in what you're about to read. At the structural level, you will notice that the following chapters, though dealing with discreet themes, are marked by quick gear shifts, the evocative idea posed and left behind, mysteries presented and left unsolved, the occasional free association, and some meaningful digressions. This is not a work in progress because it is written, done, and tied together by a thematic bow, but it is a probatory project intended to open doors.

CHAPTER 1

What Do You Mean You Can't Repeat the Past?

Dylan's Historical Universe

Any discussion of Dylan's engagement with historical traditions faces serious challenges. First, our understanding of the past, our understanding of history, is multifaceted and hard to define. There are many handbooks on how to write history, but these are intended for a very specific academic audience interested in a relatively narrow set of academic exercises, excluding an array of historical activities that inform our sense of the past. This issue is complicated further because Dylan does not subscribe to any historical "school" nor does he subscribe to any one methodology nor has he made any systematic comments on his style of historical engagement.

And yet, I do think there are ways to reconstruct some influences on Dylan's historical consciousness. I'll take cues from the man himself. This chapter offers hints, sketches, and shards of various broadly conceived historical traditions he has alluded to or belongs to by virtue of being a musician. These traditions do not add up to a coherent historical worldview but suggest a range of possible entries into the past that Dylan has at his disposal—a historical tool kit. Dylan's historical imagination, a mysterious and unconscious thing, results from the collision of these historiographical elements.

INTO THE LIBRARY, INTO THE PAST

Dylan liked staying with Ray Gooch and Chloe Kiel. The perks included a view onto Manhattan, stretches of silence, and an eclectic library. If you stood and took in all the books lining the shelves, he recalls, "you could take it all for a joke." There were books "on typography, biography, philosophy, political ideologies." Books on history too, and these were among the first mentioned in his bibliographic account: a sixteenth-century martyrology by John Foxe (*Book of Martyrs*) and a series of classical texts including Suetonius's *Twelve Caesars*, Tacitus's lectures, Pericles's *Ideal State of Democracy*, and Thucydides's *The Athenian General.*[1] The last of these struck Dylan to the core; it was "a narrative which would give you chills." Thucydides seemed untouchable. Neither the great medieval theologian Albert Magnus nor books on "the authentic American prophet" Joseph Smith cut muster in Ray's library—"This stuff pales in comparison to Thucydides, too."[2]

Like Ray and Chloe, some books in this library were make-believe. Tacitus lectures? Who knew Pericles had written a book? *The Athenian General?* These inventions are all part of the literary game played in Dylan's memoir, *Chronicles: Volume One.* Though some readers took Dylan at his word—their fault, not his—knowledge of these falsehoods only adds to the phantasmagorical quality of this imagined library scene. His creative use of a classical textual tradition does not imply ignorance of that tradition; on the contrary, playfulness implies comfort. As Harvard classicist Richard Thomas suggests, Dylan's mischievous miscues are in themselves signs of his deep interest in antiquity.[3] In this context, and for our purposes, Dylan's emphatic embrace of Thucydides, a so-called father of Western historical practice, is important. Because the ancient Greek writer seems to have been, as Thomas suggests, "at the peak of Dylan's Parnassus," it makes sense to start with him.[4]

☙

Thucydides was a warrior before he became a historian. He served as a general for Athens against the Spartan Alliance in the Peloponnesian War, an existential battle for Athenian survival. After he had been removed from charge, he wrote an account of the battle (up to 411 BC), the *History of the Peloponnesian Wars*. Apart from the story told and the potential lessons therein, Thucydides gave important pointers about how to write history. He sternly criticized credulous interpreters: "People accept quite uncritically any reports of the past they get from others, even those relating to their own country."[5] People are so uninterested in exploring the truth, he grouched, that they accept the first story they hear. Thucydides, on the other hand, claims to provide an accurate narrative by carefully parsing sources, a process helped by his aversion to exaggeration. He examined a range of accounts with appropriate skepticism and challenged his own assumptions: "I resolved not to rely in my writing on what I learned from chance sources or even on my own impressions, but both in the cases where I was present myself and in those where I depended on others I investigated every detail with the utmost concern for accuracy."[6] Moreover, he wrote in a plain style to provide "a clear view of what happened in the past."[7] For Thucydides, history should be cleansed of high tales and myths in order to render the past *as it was*.

Millennia later, when university history departments first flourished, Thucydides's work and his approach to historical writing proved resilient. In nineteenth-century Germany, where historiographical principles were influentially articulated, Thucydides attained heroic status.[8] To many, he stood out as the founder of a "scientific" school of historical writing. The most famous proponent of "scientific history" of the era, Leopold von Ranke, clearly looked back to him when formulating the basic precept that the historian should aim to describe the past "how it actually was." Thus, together with truthfulness, nineteenth-century admirers of the ancient Greek historian embraced his idealization of verisimilitude. Barthold Georg Niebuhr, another important historian of the times, emphasized both Thucydides's "reliability" and his "life-like representations."[9] These notions, as Peter Novick has shown, crossed the Atlantic to the United States and helped define American historical scholarship.[10] They have now become commonplace in the popular imagination.

The "scientific" form of history that entranced Thucydides's modern followers was coupled with a devotion to "objectivity" mediated by data (usually written sources). The fetishization of objectivity by some early professional historians and by scientific communities in the nineteenth and twentieth centuries rested on the premise that the judicious scholar could somehow remove the "self" from his (indeed, primarily *his*) investigatory and observational functions to apprehend nature.[11] In this quest, advocates of scientific history insisted on restraining from moral judgments and even predictive statements based on historical patterns.[12] And yet, even those who touted disciplinary rigor and accuracy dipped their toes in the fantastical. Though they had a strong sense of the difference between now and then, these categories nevertheless collapsed, or were stretched, because even the most punctilious historians unwittingly aspired to artistic and literary goals: they wanted to evoke an image (through words) of the past and to *re-create* lived experience insofar as language and human possibilities allowed.

For Thucydides, accuracy was at the service of utility, and utility was a result of historical repetition. What had been done would be done again. This was not by divine ordination or simple fate but because of the human condition, which assured that things would "happen again some time in the future in similar or much the same way."[13]

Dylan sometimes subscribes to a Thucydidean model of historical thinking. *Chronicles* brims with historical analysis in which, time and again, we see hints of the renewable past. From his studies of Civil War newspapers, for example, he is taken back to Rome. Plantation owners were just like people in "the Roman republic where an elite group of characters rule supposedly for the good of all." When he recalls the anxieties and the expectations surrounding the Cuban Missile Crisis, Dylan talks about how the Cuban exile community peddled the notion that "if they could get enough donations, they could take back Cuba, the old Cuba, land of plantations, sugar-cane, rice, and tobacco—patricians." Dylan curtly tells us that they wanted to reclaim the "Roman Republic."[14] Whether or not these parallels are convincing is less important than the fact that Dylan is thinking (or is claiming to think) in these homologies.

Dylan took to heart the principle that he was purportedly taught by a college professor: "If you read about Greece in the history books, you'll know all about America. Nothing that happens will puzzle you ever again. You read the history of Ancient Greece and when the Romans came in, and nothing will ever bother you about America again."[15] If you look at the past from where you stand, you will see how *things really were*, and how they will be again.

If Thucydides squawked about giving readers the truth, he did not deny the creative elements of his narrative. Gestures toward a method of source criticism and rationality aside, he nevertheless emphasized that his work maintained traditional literary and rhetorical qualities, if not the noxious fables of his predecessors. Thucydides informed readers that because it was hard to recall speeches that he witnessed (by warriors, generals, and such), or for others whom he consulted to recall what they had heard, the oratorical feats he included were partly the product of his imagination: "What I have set down is how I think each of them would have expressed what was most appropri-ate in the particular circumstances, while staying as close as possible to the overall intention of what was actually said."[16] Though Thu-cydides did not simply make things up, he didn't fret about sticking to the facts or shirk from massaging them in a historically informed way. Set speeches and debates are the axes around which his narra-tive moves and how meaning is developed from start to finish.

Some would argue that the rhetorical impulse never went away. As the literary critic Hayden White would influentially (and con-troversially) argue, even the promoters of historical scientism in the nineteenth century could not escape literary forms in their nar-rative structures.[17] They were not too different from their Greek predecessors. In the wake of such a stance, plenty of modern and postmodern commentary has tended to question, based on a range of skeptical and relativistic stances, the "truth claims" made by historians.[18] Save for time travel, can we ever have the sources to know what happened in the past? Can historical narratives ever be anything but the subjective musings of the historian? Some suggest real historical figures are fundamentally narrated into being, and in turn can (must?) be read much as we might a fictional character. From a different perspective, writer and semiotician Umberto Eco has pointed out that the reader of a fictional work must accept the truth of a novel's characters and thus knows more about them than they would about a "real" human being.[19]

This interpenetration of fact and fiction, of literature and history, brings us back to Dylan. Dylan understands Thucydides's history as a commentary on language. In *Chronicles* he says that Thucydides wrote about "how words in his time have changed from their ordinary meaning, how actions and opinions can be altered in the blink of an eye."[20]

Linguistic flexibility is at the core of a famous scene in *The Peloponnesian Wars*. As the first year of combat between Sparta and Athens ended, Athenians reflected on their glorious dead. At this point, the Athenian general, Pericles, delivers his famous "Funeral Oration," one of the most effective set pieces of the whole history and one that smacked Dylan in the face. It hit him so hard that, as mentioned before, he playfully refers to it as an independent work, *The Ideal State of Democracy*. Dylan names it this because the deaths of soldiers are praised as reflections of Athenian glory and are promoted as exemplary sacrifices of individual interests to the common good.

The speech also, and repeatedly, comments on the distinction between things said and things done. Pericles fears the first might triumph over the latter. The speech starts by insisting that dead soldiers need not be praised by words but should be praised by action, "otherwise we risk the good name of many on the persuasive powers of one man, who may speak well or badly."[21] Elsewhere, he makes a point dear to Thucydides's own heart: Athenians "need no Homer to sing our praises, nor any moment to gratify us for the moment with lines which may fail the test of history, for we have forced every land and sea to yield to our daring and we have established everywhere lasting memorials of our power for good will."[22] To pin hopes on individuals and their words would be madness given the frailties of both.

Pericles's speech is a preface, a foreshadowing, of crucial narrative points of Thucydides's history that reveal precisely what Dylan noticed about the changeability of "ordinary meanings." When Dylan gives us his thumbnail interpretation of Thucydides, he is thinking about the dramatic events of book 3, where the author discusses the internal strife among the Corcyraeans caught as they were between Athens and Sparta. These were, to put it simply, crazy times. "War," Thucydides says, "is a violent master: it robs us of the means of providing easily for our daily life and needs, and it usually generates passions to match our circumstances."[23] In this context, norms of society and values are overturned; what was once thought unworthy becomes worthy, what was once thought to be bad is now good. "Men assumed the right to reverse the usual values in the application of words to action."[24] As Dylan interprets this phrase, words used remain the same, but men changed their meaning. This can happen quickly, "at the blink of an eye."[25]

Dylan had clearly been thinking along these lines for a while. In a 1985 interview with Toby Creswell for *Rolling Stone Australia*, Dylan makes the point in response to a question about anticommunist sentiment. Dylan says, "People need somebody to hate, you've got to hate something. . . . The Early Christians were like communists. The Roman Empire treated the Early Christians the same way the Western World treats communists." Creswell prods: "So it doesn't really change?" Dylan answers by evoking the theme of shifting nomenclature: "No, things don't [change], it's just got a different name on it. There's always someone you're told you've got to step on so you can rise up a little higher."[26] Here we have Dylan, knowingly or not, tying a nice Thucydidean bow, conjoining the notion that history repeats itself with the sense that the names applied to those continuities are manipulated.

Just as Dylan might be swept up in Thucydides's strident self-confidence, he might well end up in netherworld of doubt. If the significance of words can so easily be changed, what then of the historian? Eight years after *Chronicles* was released, Dylan would sound off on history writing and the fragility of truth. In a *Rolling Stone* interview linked to the release of *Tempest* (2012) Dylan muses,

> History's a funny thing, isn't it? History can be changed. The past can be changed and distorted and used for propaganda purposes. Things we've been told happened might not have happened at all. And things that we were told that didn't happen actually might have happened. Newspapers do it all the time; history books do it all the time. Everybody changes the past in their own way. It's habitual, you know? We always see things the way they really weren't, or we see them the way we want to see them. We can't change the present or the future. We can only change the past, and we do it all the time.[27]

Dylan's skepticism is ultimately of a piece with Thucydides. It's not so much that history must be bunk, but that its writers and performers make it so. Dylan evokes Shelby Foote's gargantuan narrative of the Civil War and says that he and Civil War reenactors were seeing things from a distance.[28] They weren't actually there and couldn't really know anything. He advises that if we want to know the truth or "what it was all about" we should look at period newspapers: "You'll see things that you won't believe." He insists that "it's nothing like what you read in the history books." A gap of logic rears its head, because if one accepts the impossibility of being in Grant's shoes, Dylan nevertheless claims this impossibility will somehow be mitigated by reading newspapers.[29] The point, though, still stands—if you read those papers correctly, you will know what *actually* happened.

Just as Dylan places Thucydides on a pedestal, he does the same to Homer. Thucydides would shudder. Dylan does not (necessarily) conflate the work of a poet and the work of a historian writing narrative nonfiction, but Homer, and more specifically *The Odyssey*, surely imparted a *sense* of the past.

Scholars have suggested that Homer's epic is among the first to articulate a modern historical consciousness. Indeed, one scene in particular has been highlighted along these lines. In book 8, Odysseus, who after the Trojan War has been tossed here and there, finds himself in the court of Alcinous, king of the Phaeacians. There, he is feted and as part of the entertainment Demodocus sings the story of the war that Odysseus himself had survived. As he listens, he breaks. He has to hide his face to hide his tears, "clutching his flaring sea-blue cape in both powerful hands."[30] Why is he crying? Classicist François Hartog has suggested that the moment is one of "self-estrangement," when the difference between "I" now and "me" then creates a tearful rupture.[31] The poem recited within the poem is no longer that of a one-dimensional event, says Hartog, but one couched in the pastness of the past.

Dylan does not necessarily think about the Odyssey in these esoteric ways, but he does talk about the alienation resulting from a man's quest to get back home. In his Nobel Lecture, he lingers on *The Odyssey* as a source of inspiration, and especially on the theme of Odysseus's return, which ends up being less sweet than Homer's hero imagined. As Dylan would have it: "When he gets back home, things aren't any better. Scoundrels have moved in and are taking advantage of his wife's hospitality. And there's too many of 'em. And though he's greater than them all and the best at everything—best carpenter, best hunter, best expert on animals, best seaman—his courage won't save him, but his trickery will." So, what he returns to is far different from what he left, something Dylan contemplated in "Sugar Baby" from *"Love and Theft"* (2001), where he writes, "You can't turn back you can't come back, sometimes we push too far / One day you'll open up your eyes and you'll see where we are."

When Odysseus and his wife are reunited, all that's left are the stories of an unshared past. As Dylan tells it, "He [Odysseus] was nobody. And when it's all said and done, when he's home at last, he sits with his wife, and he tells her the stories." On Dylan's telling, then, the poem is very much about the dissolution of experiences that can only be called back to life through narrative, but only so far.

Ultimately, Dylan feels himself more Homer than Thucydides, as a singer of songs. At the end of his Nobel Lecture he quotes the *Iliad*: "I return once again to Homer, who says, 'Sing in me, oh Muse, and through me tell the story.'" But what is that sung story? It is something that "lives in the land of the living," to be experienced in the real world, with the potential to "transport me into a world I'd never known." This "new world" was not fantastical because, as Dylan explains, listening to folk and blues repertoires birthed palpable realities:

> You know what it's all about. Takin' the pistol out and puttin' it back in your pocket. Whippin' your way through traffic, talkin' in the dark. You know that Stagger Lee was a bad man and that Frankie was a good girl. You know that Washington is a bourgeois town and you've heard the deep-pitched voice of John the Revelator and you saw the Titanic sink in a boggy creek. And you're pals with the wild Irish rover and the wild colonial boy. You heard the muffled drums and the fifes that played lowly. You've seen the lusty Lord Donald stick a knife in his wife, and a lot of your comrades have been wrapped in white linen.[32]

And so, it seems that the muse of song does not take us too far from the muse of history proper. A few years before the Nobel Lecture, Dylan contemplated the subject, saying that "a songwriter doesn't care about what's truthful. What he cares about is what should've happened, what could've happened. That's its own kind of truth."[33] Just like Homer, just like Thucydides (the rhetorician), the modern songster can produce a verisimilar past edging toward veracity itself.

ALL THE FREAKS

With pounding, out-of-tune, B-minor chords, like vaudeville flourishes gone wrong, and the ghostly howl of an organ, Mr. Jones, pencil in his pocket, enters a strange room. A place full of life, all questions, no answers. He sees a geek who thinks he's a freak. The sword swallower kneels and gives him back his throat. The one-eyed midget screams "no!" and asks him for milk.

Dylan's "Ballad of a Thin Man" from *Highway 61 Revisited* (1965) is a vicious takedown of everyone trying to figure Dylan out. He places Mr. Jones—the archetypal square—in a place he will find disorienting. We might be confused too, but not the singer, maybe not Dylan either.

The weirdness of carnival culture has long lit Dylan's imagination and inflected his identity. Early on in his career, when he created and re-created his biography at will, when he insisted that his "past is so complicated you wouldn't even believe it," Dylan often included carnival stints.[34] In 1961 he told Israel "Izzy" Young, owner of the influential Folklore Center in Greenwich Village, that he had "started playing in carnivals when he was 14, with guitar and piano."[35] On a radio interview leading up to his first album, *Bob Dylan* (1962), Dylan told Cynthia Gooding that he'd worked at a carnival on and off for six years as a jack-of-all-trades: a cleanup boy, ride runner, and more.

He has claimed that these experiences were transformational. At one carnival there were "midgets and all that kind of stuff. There's one lady in there, really bad shape. Like, her skin had been all burned and she was a little baby, didn't grow right, so she was like a freak. All these people would pay money to see. That really sort of got me. That's the funny thing about them, I know how those people think. They want to sell you stuff. . . . They want to make you have two thoughts. They want to make you think that they don't feel bad about themselves and also, they want to make you feel sorry for them. I always liked that."[36] Dylan clearly admired the performance style of freaks and its sophistication. He tells Gooding that he learned how to sing under circus tents.

Fifty years later he returned to the carnival, the sideshow, and its virtues. In an interview with Bill Flanagan, he recalls being attracted to traveling performers: "The sideshow performers . . . Miss Europe, Quasimodo, the Bearded lady, the half-man half woman, the deformed and bent, Atlas the Dwarf, the fire-eaters, the teachers and preachers . . ."[37] From this grab bag of backroad travelers, he learned something about individuality. He came to understand things about dignity, about how "to stay within yourself."[38]

High tales about the carnival might have been a result of some childhood experiences, but they are of a piece with the cultural moment of the early sixties. The carnival, in all its grittiness, was attaining renewed stature, especially among the young counterculture set. This was the moment when, for example, Tod Browning's film *Freaks* (1932) became a cult classic after years of neglect and derision for depicting a vulgar love affair between a "midget" and a "normal" woman who ends up a monstrous feathered creature. By the sixties, at least among a certain crowd, this all seemed less like a peek into the gutters of humanity and more about the marginalized, the misused and confused.[39]

Whatever the reason, Dylan's soft spot for the carnival aesthetic has never wavered. *"Love and Theft"* (2001) is all about old musical forms and sounds, and it is tellingly wrapped in the carnivalesque. "Honest with Me," a gutbucket blues, talks about the Siamese twins coming to town, people throwing baseball bats in the air, women with faces like teddy bears, women who give Dylan (or the singer) the creeps. Throughout the album there is a penchant for the topsy-turvy, the world seen through cracked glasses.

It is no coincidence that some of the original photos for the project by David Gahr catch Dylan in one of the iconic American carnivals: Coney Island. In one of these, Dylan looks like someone from an old-time cowboy band next to an old ad for a ninety-eight-pound man, in another he stands in front of a vitrine with clown costumes, and in another next to the "World's Smallest Woman Exhibit." He even cracks a thin smile holding a water gun at the "Balloon Water Race Game." Although these pictures did not make it on the album, in them we sense a faint evocation of the cover art for the first *Basement Tapes* release (1975), where clowns, fire-eaters, little people, and many others intermingle in a raucous scene and among whom Dylan is air-bowing a mandolin.

The carnival has reappeared recently in *Masked and Anonymous*, a feature film written with Larry Charles (of *Seinfeld*, *Curb your Enthusiasm*, and *Borat!* fame). Jack Fate (Bob Dylan)—a washed-up singer—has been called to perform a charity concert as a last resort. Johnny

Sweetheart (John Goodman), the show's deadbeat producer, introduces him to some of the players that will round out the event as they pile into his trailer. The screenplay describes them as "a motley crew of freaks and weirdos."[40] Sweetheart barks: "Just the greatest human menagerie since the Stone Age at our services . . . Jean Darkness, the Rubber Girl, Eddie Quicksand with Milo, the Great El Mundo with Ella the Fortune Teller and our shooting gallery of beloved world leaders, John Paul Deuce, Mahatma Gandhi, and our own beloved Abraham Lincoln." The screenplay points out Fate's "discomfort" at the sight, but in the movie he looks on with a smirk.

The historical figures are striking. The idea of having these lookalikes come in, most of them long dead, is a reminder that if at the carnival a big-moled lady can tell your future, it is also a place to observe the past.

Sweetheart, a corpulent, sweat-drenched high talker and bottom drinker revives the past. Due to a situation partly beyond his control, he is forced to bring Jack Fate out of his prison hole, a relic of a musical culture that had faded. Although Fate is a last choice, Sweetheart justifies his selection with grandiloquent gestures and most-likely overstated claims that this third-rank celebrity was once the voice of his generation. The bigness and brashness of the character reflect Dylan and Charles's conception of Sweetheart as a modern P. T. Barnum. Barnum, like Sweetheart, was also a hustler who trafficked in history. He was the Thucydides of tall tales and entertainment in the nineteenth century.

Barnum's first break into the sideshow business involved a nursemaid. As he described Joice Heth, she could have been a talking corpse. Said to be 161 years old, she "might almost as well have been called a thousand years old as any other age." Heth was immobile, almost ossified. She could move one arm fairly well, but "her lower limbs were fixed in their position and could not be straightened." Aside from her prodigious age and mummy-like countenance, she proved an important attraction because of her connection to that greatest of American generals, the first president of the United States, her "protégé," as Barnum calls him, a boy she called "little George."[41] As an advertisement from the *New York Sun* (1835) put it, Heth was "the slave of Augustine Washington (the father of Gen. Washington) and was the first person who put cloths [*sic*] on the unconscious infant who was destined to lead our heroic fathers on to glory, to victory, and to freedom." Viewers who came to see her would witness a "marvelous relic of antiquity."[42] Heth was an object worthy of something like veneration and, more importantly, she created a direct, physical link to something greater than herself. Heth connected citizens who came to see her directly with the founding of America.

That Barnum's first big splash reached back to the origins of American history is not coincidental. Kevin Young, in his masterful examination of falsehoods and deceptions in American culture, has pointed out that "Barnum and others used bunk to connect the audience to a history—usually a grand, American one—that it desperately wished were true."[43] These stories often hinged on the exotic "other," strange creatures that hearkened back to a past that was at once familiar and unfamiliar, marked by attributes of recognizable primitiveness that were perceived as inversionary of modern, white society. Especially within the context of burgeoning Darwinism and its vision(s) of natural history, society could bear witness to remnants of a savage past, of primal origins. Examples of this sensibility abound: the Aztec Children (Maximo and Bartola) and Krao, Darwin's "missing link," to name just two attractions.[44]

The historical and, indeed, genealogical nature of these aberrant bodies was not an invention of the nineteenth century. The carnival and museums of wonder bastardized broadly accepted intellectual traditions going back at least as far back as the cabinets of curiosities in the sixteenth and seventeenth centuries in which bodies—alive or mummified—could be shown in efforts to display humans as a part of a broader natural history. These efforts were related to traditions that saw in "monsters" a way to understand the horizons of nature, the significance of its exceptions.[45]

Of course, not everyone accepted what the carnival peddled. An increasingly potent scientific discourse made Barnum's wonders seem unacceptable to the cognoscenti. Thus, as popular as Joice Heth had become, she also became exemplary of deceit, or as one contemporary put it, "She was the veriest imposter that ever the ingenuity of cunning Yankees humbugged the public with."[46] Barnum did not mind this sort of critique. In fact, he encouraged doubt and was even the first to plant it. Great showman that he was, he reveled in the controversy, making the debate about purported veracity an end in itself. Indeed, the tension between verity and verisimilitude was an important factor in audience enjoyment. While the spectacle seemed real, it was (often) simultaneously perceived as fake, and in that contradiction lay the aesthetic value, the enjoyment, the affective experience of the show.[47]

As a child, Dylan likely saw Edmund Goulding's chilling noire *Nightmare Alley* (1947), a movie that is fixated on origins. The movie tells the story of Stan Carlisle (Tyrone Powers), a carney who makes it big and falls hard after taking his con act too far. The first scene shows a barker calling people to his attraction, which he says is "only in the interest of education and science." He is presenting the Geek— the same Geek mentioned in "Ballad of a Thin Man"—who has "puzzled the foremost scientists in Europe and America. Is he the missing link? Is he man or beast?" We don't actually see the beast, but a backdrop shows a crouched Neanderthal about to eat a live chicken. The barker throws live chickens beneath the stage from where the audience hears a dying squawk before being distracted by a flamethrower. Like all the acts presented in the movie, the Geek is a hoax, but there is at the same time something "true" about these hoaxes. Later we discover that Stan himself becomes the Geek as he descends into near-subhuman alcoholism. This strange world of forgery and debauchery allows a space for an imagined human-beast hybrid that in the minds of the crowd, and in the logic of the film, reflect something fundamental that may or may not be real.

Stan's fall gets at something about the human core and the mysterious origins of mankind. The audience may not be witnessing what the barker claims, but the broken man nevertheless displays primal impulses, something about our basest traits.

It's hard to imagine that a young and impressionable Dylan would not have intuited this. From an early age, and from various cultural materials, including carnivals themselves and representations of the carnival, Dylan would have become aware that it was a laboratory for understanding a kind of natural history.

The carnival and its sideshows produced music histories as well. Joice Heth, for example, was a singer. A notice from the *Philadelphia Inquirer* of 1835 tells readers, "She has been a member of the Baptist Church one hundred and sixteen years, and can rehearse many hymns and sing them according to former custom."[48] So apart from her connection with little George, she also enlivened a religious past and old-style singing.

Heth is perhaps a remarkable "specimen," but the presence of an aural past was not unique to her story. When Dylan recalls his experiences at carnivals, he underlines the availability of old-time music. He lists among the acts he saw there "bluegrass singers, the black cowboy . . . the blues singer."[49] Strikingly, in *Chronicles* he says that he "saw one of the last blackface minstrel shows at a country carnival."[50] Barnum, it should be noted, was one of the first big-time commercial exploiters of the blackface extravaganzas.

This nod at minstrelsy confirms that Dylan sometimes sees the carnival as a place for exploring musical beginnings. Toward the end of *Masked and Anonymous*, at the moment when Jack Fate is set to take the stage, he enters a tent with a carnival sign showing a "man eating chicken" and sees a suited man eating a bucket of fried chicken, an inversion of the Geek image mentioned above from Golding's film. The scene then shifts as Fate climbs up to the rafters and observes the bustle beneath. From behind appears a man in blackface with banjo in hand: Oscar Vogel (Ed Harris), whose name evokes one of the most important white minstrel entrepreneurs of the late nineteenth century, John Vogel. Oscar asks, "Do you know me?" Fate responds, "You look familiar." Vogel tells him, "I was the star of the show, one of the biggest stars. I was one of your father's favorite performers once." An earlier version of the screenplay imagined a slightly different encounter, though the point is much the same. Vogel meets Dylan on the soundstage where he was to perform and reminds him that once he was the biggest star, and that "[your] father would bring you when you were a child. You'd play your guitar. Sing a song."[51] This exchange encapsulates the theme I've underlined so far: Jack Fate (Dylan) identifies this carnival space with the ghosts of the past, indeed, with the ghosts of his forefathers—in the movie, literally his father—who had enabled his performance tradition. As David Yaffe has put it, the scene shows Vogel "taunting Dylan's character Jack Fate to remember the burnt cork origins of his musical identity."[52]

The real Dylan has talked about the carnival as a place of bizarre remembrance. During the last days of carney shows, he recalls seeing "guys in blackface, George Washington in blackface, Napoleon wearing blackface . . . stuff that didn't make sense at the time, but actually it did, I probably retained a lot of it, because when I started writing songs, I started subliminally writings a lot of songs which I probably wouldn't have attempted to even think about unless I had some concept of that type of reality of mixing genres and ages and different historical figures from the past."[53] The carnival collapses time, turns history inside out and upside down, makes it feel strange. The great men of history, the white heroes from the history books, are re-etched in that world of wonders, parading in feigned blackness, revealing a submerged history of the West that has been about racial subjugation and mimicry.

Here's the rub: the carnival was both a place of historical recreation and re-creation, with origin stories abounding, and with a disorienting effect (as far as Dylan is concerned) constituted by intermixing artifacts of the past with performances in the present.

FOLK ANTIQUARIANISM

When Dylan was inducted into the Rock and Roll Hall of Fame (1988), he singled out Alan Lomax for praise and thanks. By that time Lomax had long attained legendary status after years of traveling here, there, and everywhere lugging clunky recording equipment to "record the world," as a recent biographer has put it.[54] Alan and his father John before him were interested in maintaining traditions of the folk, identifying the oldest, purest versions of those traditions, and conserving them through recordings and transcriptions, today held at the Library of Congress, the Briscoe Center in Austin, and elsewhere.

As an inveterate collector of old music, Alan Lomax, even more than his father, can be considered an "antiquarian." The antiquarian, as opposed to the historian, has over time been perceived as the intellectual inferior, interested only in objects, in surfaces, not in constructing coherent narratives of the past or deciphering any deep meaning of the objects they hoard. Such an uncharitable take is overblown, and scholars today see the emergence of modern historical methods as deeply entwined with antiquarianism, which required not only obsessive-compulsive acquisitional habits but also a sophisticated understanding of the objects (or sources) being collected and their meaning *within the context* in which they were created.

The Lomaxes were part of an old tradition of collecting songs going back at least to the so-called Age of Enlightenment, when men opened their ears to the sounds of people perceived at a remove from urbanity and modern society. Scholars went to them with pen and paper in hand to transcribe their "ancient" poetry. Successors in this quest would make use of the latest technologies to capture songs in recordings and in doing so essentially reversed the traditional antiquarian pursuit: in ages past collectors sought objects and rendered them (almost) immaterial through drawings or other visual media, but with recording technologies and ultimately the production of records, scholars and trawlers created tactile materials out of "nothing."

The act of collecting and publishing "traditional" music was always an interpretive act premised on its cultural significance. Indeed, the long tradition of folklore and its collecting habits were intimately linked with nationalist sentiments radiating from eighteenth-century Europe. At that time, great thinkers such as the theologian-philosopher-proto-folklorist Johann Gottfried Herder would urge the collection of folk materials, mostly from old manuscripts, that would help moderns "reflect on their [the songs'] context, their times, and the vital way they touched real people." Just as important, old music would help us understand the constitution of a people: "The Language, sound, and content of the old songs shape the way a people think, thereby leaving its mark on the nation."[55]

The Lomaxes' spirit of collection was influenced by a historicist impulse bred, to an extent, in academic halls. During his graduate studies, John came under the influence of George Lyman Kittredge, a scholar with a specialty in medieval and Renaissance literature, who also became a powerhouse in American folklore studies as the successor to Francis James Child, whose extraordinarily influential *English and Scottish Popular Ballads,* originally published in five volumes, he edited into a very popular one-volume edition. Although Kittridge would promote a public awareness of American traditions themselves—he would encourage John to establish the Texas Folklore Society—his most direct influence may have been through a Harvard course (inherited from Child) on the ballad, which John took.[56] Kittredge would promote a transhistorical interpretation of the ballad by gathering regional examples without sacrificing specificity. His method played with temporality by at once emphasizing timeless elements of the genre *and* cultivating a historical impulse to discover the *origins* of specific musical and cultural traditions.

Alan Lomax was wholly his father's son, but he eventually branched off and established his own intellectual links. He came under the spell of anthropology and ethnography, especially as established by Franz Boas, the famed Columbia University professor. The Boasian influence came directly from the man himself, with whom Alan maintained correspondence; from Boas's students, who were Alan's professors during graduate studies at Columbia; and in his later exchanges with the great anthropologist (and Boas acolyte) Margaret Mead.[57] Perhaps most importantly, at barely twenty years old, Alan developed a close relationship with one of Boas's most famous students, author and ethnographer Zora Neale Hurston.

Boas promoted an explicitly historicist methodology. Instead of assessing cultures through eternal categories or universal characteristics, history should be a starting point for understanding present behaviors and beliefs. As George Stocking explains, "Only through history could cultural laws be established." Moreover, for Boas, different cultures could not be ranked according to Eurocentric assumptions. Again, according to Stocking, cultural assessments could result only from the "empirical study of the actual distribution of phenomena, and the collection and publication of large masses of data . . . to provide the basis for future inductive study."[58] A version of this precept was handed down to Lomax by Hurston, who, in terms of Black cultural life, encouraged Alan to "see further than the surface of things." As she told his father, John, "There has been too much loose talk and conclusions argued without sufficient proof. So I tried to make him [Alan] do and see clearly so that no one can come after him and refute him."[59] More important than her encouragement of systematic research and observation, Hurston was a promoter of (rural) folk Black culture and its music in counterpoint to an important part of the Black intelligentsia of the early twentieth century who wanted to create a new modernist Black art. Her emphasis—and this was shared with Lomax—was on showcasing "authentic" Black culture, uncovering ancient voices and primordial roots, which were as powerful as anything in any elite Western canon.[60]

The quest for origins led the Lomaxes to Black traditions. For John, whose interests, like those of his intellectual forefathers, hinged on the English roots of Americana, Black dialects preserved elements of the language imparted by early American planters to their slaves.[61] This impulse to use Black people as a key to understand the most antique aspects of white America over time evolved into a sense (among some) that Black culture was quintessentially American, and so Alan came to recognize, though the sentiment had been articulated well before him by doyens of high as much as low culture, that Black spirituals and the blues were "the best art that our country has produced."[62]

☙

Dylan sees a connection between history and collecting. In *Chronicles*, the chapter that deals with his own origins, his first awakening to folk musical culture, is marked by saturation. In reminiscing about his earliest days in the shadow of the Great War, he thinks about his uncles who had been soldiers and, more specifically, he recalled the things that they had brought back: "Uncle Paul, Maurice, Jack, Max, Louis, Vernon and others had all gone off to the Philippines, Anzio, Sicily, North Africa, France, and Belgium. They brought back mementos and keepsakes—a straw Japanese cigarette case, German bread bag, a British enameled mug, German dust goggles, British fighting knife, a German Luger pistol—all kinds of junk."[63] As mentioned earlier, when Dylan made it to New York, he describes (an imagined) library in the apartment of (imagined) friends, chalk-full of books that he deems transformational: "The place had an overpowering presence of literature and you couldn't help but lose your passion for dumbness."[64] In recalling the Village music scene he talks in splurges of names: "Van Ronk, Stookey, Romney, Hal Waters, Paul Clayton, Luke Faust, Len Chandler . . ."[65] He remembers with awe the cardroom at the Kettle of Fish Tavern in the Village: "A frantic atmosphere—all kinds of characters talking fast, moving fast—some debonair some rakish. Literary types with black beards, grim-faced intellectuals—eclectic girls, non home-maker types. The kind of people who come from nowhere and go right back into it—a pistol-packing rabbi, a snaggle-toothed girl with a big crucifix between her breasts. . . . Some people even had titles—'The Man Who Made History,' 'The Link Between the Races,'" and more.[66] These are all the memories (real or invented) of a man who thinks in lists, a professional gatherer of faces and images that are sooner or later set free through his work.

The myth of Dylan the folkie, when he turned from Little Richard and Chuck Berry to Woody Guthrie and Pete Seeger, is filled with collector tropes. There are the stories of record stealing and all the (overstated when not plain false) narratives of travel and wandering linked to song gathering. This persona was established early in his career, and so it is no surprise that Oscar Brand in a 1961 radio interview described Dylan as a voracious gatherer. He announced to the listening audience that Dylan's upcoming concert at Carnegie Chapter Hall would feature "songs that he's collected from many people." Brand then suggests that Dylan has learned so many songs that he must have forgotten plenty along the way. Dylan responds, "Oh yeah, I learned . . . I forgot quite a few, I guess, and once when I forget them I usually heard the name of them and looked them up in some book and learned them again."[67]

By all accounts, Dylan has a prodigious memory for things musical, so his early song collecting had lasting influence even after he left his strictly folk years behind. One testament to this are the Basement Tapes, once-cherished bootlegs of recordings made in the late sixties on the cheap and in private spaces by Dylan with a group that would soon be called The Band. The recordings include new compositions ("Quinn the Eskimo," "This Wheel's on Fire," "I Shall Be Released," etcetera) emerging out of a vast sea of older songs across genres (folk, blues, country, and even Tin Pan Alley) that together have been interpreted as a roadmap to an "old, weird, America." Ultimately, what Dylan and his companions created was not unlike what Lomax and his contemporary collectors produced. Indeed, Robbie Robertson, in retrospect, sees in the depth and breadth of their explorations, and in the unpolished rawness of the tapes themselves, something akin to "field recordings."[68]

Dylan's musical interests have evolved into a more formal curatorship. It is now a stamp of musical credibility to talk about stars from Dylan's generation as quasiarchivists and scholars, but Dylan perhaps more than most is often labeled a musicologist. This is partly of his own doing. His persona of collector, audiophile, and music scholar (not to mention showman) has found lasting public expression in his Sirius XM Radio show, *Theme Time Radio Hour* (2006–9, with a one-off reboot in 2020), which features songs on any given theme— "Cops & Robbers," "Numbers Eleven & Up," "Weather," etcetera. Although the quirky program might seem peripheral to Dylan's work in general, such an expansive project (over one hundred episodes) should be considered, as John Hay says, "central, rather than ancillary, to his oeuvre."[69] The whole show, though on satellite radio, is populated by ghosts. In terms of content, DJ Dylan spins "records" from an array of musical traditions that influenced him, and almost all the tracks are old. In presenting an American musical past, Dylan evokes programming by previous promoters of musical traditions, including, for example, Alan Lomax's *American Folk Songs, Back Where I Come From,* and *The Wellsprings of Music.* Dylan never says as much, but his show, like its predecessors, is as much about enjoyment as it is about recovering something more essential about America's musical and thus cultural past, à la Herder. Dylan is in the game of gathering and repackaging musical artifacts for digital translation and diffusion.

DREAMING OF SAINT AUGUSTINE

When Dylan returned to music making after a motorcycle accident in 1966, he had the Bible in hand. Packed with over sixty biblical allusions, Dylan himself would call *John Wesley Harding* (1967) "the first biblical rock album."[70] If the album is proof of the growing importance of scripture in his life—his mother would tell reporters that the Bible was the centerpiece of his library—it reveals extrabiblical religious interests as well.

In one of the record's simplest songs, Dylan evokes a vision of Saint Augustine, likely the fourth/fifth-century bishop of the North African city of Hippo, but (just) possibly the seventh-century missionary to England. "I Dreamed I Saw St. Augustine" draws inspiration from an old worker's ballad with poetry by Alfred Hayes and music by Earl Robinson, "I Dreamed I Saw Joe Hill." While the Hayes/Robinson number commemorates a union organizer executed on trumped-up murder charges, in Dylan's hands a meditation on an important labor movement symbol turns into the story of a spiritual martyr figure who inspires conversion. There may be glue that binds these two figures, but for now what matters is the gulf.

The singer sees Saint Augustine in a lifelike dream, as if he were actually there. He is dressed in a coat of gold, "searching for the very souls / whom already have been sold." He preaches unto kings and queens and proselytizes among the many. Augustine dies a martyr for doing so, and the singer sees himself among the murderers. That terrible fact awakens him and forces the singer to contemplate his own sin. He is left to bow his head and cry.

The song evokes an important historical tradition: hagiography, a form of life writing that tells of saints and martyrs of the church. To take one prominent example, John Foxe's *Book of Martyrs*, which Dylan mentioned as being in the Kiels's library discussed above, describes the horrors inflicted on English Protestants by English Catholics during the sixteenth century, in part to attack the confessional enemy but also to fortify believers by providing examples of good Christian piety and sufferance for Christ. Different religious traditions deal with martyrs and saints differently, but Dylan's song points to a sort of mysticism that transcends specific labels. The song itself is not a true hagiographical exercise in that it does not relate or really claim to relate Augustine's life in full, nor is it an "accurate" description of Augustine's life, as neither saint by that name was martyred. It is, however, a song about the effects of martyrdom and martyrs on believers—the tears they elicit and the internal conversions they can facilitate, as they did for the dreamer.

Dylan has assimilated the martyr story and the martyr type as a miraculous being who overcomes time and space. A glance back at "I Dreamed I Saw Joe Hill" helps flesh out this nuance. In it, the singer sees Joe Hill as if he were alive, but there is no suggestion that this dream is anything but that, a function of the imagination. Joe Hill tells the singer/dreamer that he is not dead, but this trope is used to emphasize the dream vision as a metaphor for labor rights: "From San Diego up to Maine / In every mine and mill / Where working folks defend their rights / It's there you find Joe Hill." Dylan's song is not written in the same rhetorical register because it tells a story of an individual encounter with a holy figure and the transformative powers therein. While "Joe Hill" stands in for all good fighting workers, Saint Augustine is a catalyst for individual spiritual reform.

If "I Dreamed I Saw St. Augustine" speaks of an immediate and dramatic conversion, Dylan has also explored a more gradualist path toward that same end. This is nowhere clearer, as Timothy Hampton has brilliantly discussed, than in "Every Grain of Sand," the last track on the third album of his Christian trilogy, *Shot of Love* (1981).[71] In it Dylan grapples with the multivectored experience of conversion, which calls for the acknowledgement of past sin and its rejection. If archetypes of Christian conversion such as Saint Augustine, who famously renounced Manichaeism for Christianity after a definitive spiritual event, can turn their backs on their past completely, the singer cannot. His spiritual transition is drenched in tears and seems to be a struggle between enlightenment and despair. He wants to turn away from the past, but this is merely a desire. As he goes on, he reflects on the grip of an overbearing past weighing so heavily on him that goodness, or even a sense of goodness, has been smothered. The resolution of this struggle is left ultimately in God's hands; it is God's light that lessens the pain wrought by memory. It is the knowledge of providence that provides some clarity, if not resolution, and in the end the singer experiences the pull of predestination: "I am hanging on the balance of the reality of man / Like every sparrow falling, like every grain of Sand." In an alternate version of the song, he replaces the "reality of man" with a rhythmically more effective line in which he says he is hanging in the balance "of a perfect, finished plan." In any case, the song grapples with the traumatizing experience of secular time—everyday life, past and present—and the possibility eternals of salvation.

Songs needn't be revelatory of individual experiences, but Dylan was, for a little while in the late seventies and early eighties, not shy about sharing his own conversion story. As he told an audience in Syracuse, New York, he had been tapped on the shoulder by

Jesus, who asked, "Bob, why are you resisting me?" Dylan quickly responded, "I'm not resisting you!" Jesus asked him then if he was going to follow him, and Dylan didn't quite know what to say before being admonished, "When you're not following me you are resisting me."[72] It's unclear whether Dylan intended this dialogue to be taken literally, but it is very clear that he wanted to have people understand that he had had a mystical experience. In a previous show he told of how he picked up a cross that someone had thrown on stage, and he would later claim that its powers were life changing. During a time of trouble and despair he decided he needed something but wasn't sure what until he looked into his pocket and saw the crucifix.[73] It is said that on that night when he found it, he felt the presence of Jesus. While there is some debate about the account's truthfulness, Dylan has unequivocally stated that "Jesus did appear to me as King of Kings, and Lord of Lords."[74]

In the sudden or gradual path toward conversion, the divisions between past, present, and future are blurred. Within Christianity and Judaism, rich theological traditions draw lines between the "City of God" and the "City of Man," between body and soul, the first subject to decay and the other, at least from certain theological perspectives, eternal and one with God. The realm of the divine, according to some, has no real beginning or end, while the terrestrial realm has a definite beginning (creation) and will also have an end, which in some configurations will arrive with Armageddon or, as Dylan writes more prosaically in "Things Have Changed," "if the Bible is right, the world will explode." And yet, while secular time and sacred time are distinct, their significance is mutually reinforcing. Existence means little without a sense of divine eternity. More importantly, Dylan seems to suggest that God is there to intervene, to meld the permanent with the passing.

When Dylan was deep in study with the Vineyard Fellowship, an evangelical congregation in California, at the end of the seventies, he dug deeper into scripture and joined millions in exploring popular writings on end times. Most importantly, he seems to have come under the spell of Hal Lindsey, a self-proclaimed "Bible prophecy teacher" and author of several popular books, including *The Late Great Planet Earth* and *Satan Is Alive and Well on Planet Earth*, both of which Dylan devoured.[75] In the first of these, Lindsey describes the prophetic messages in scripture that spoke of the Second Coming and how they were linked to the State of Israel. The second describes the workings of Satan on earth as a warning to all who have been caught in his evil snares. Readers interested in Lindsey's type of prophetic talk will have to go to the source, but for now it's worth underlining how he understands the presence of the holy in the realm of human time and in everyday life.

Prophecies are fundamentally about the future, but they are also words spoken in time and can be assessed only in retrospect as historical acts (the prophetic utterance). Because scripture foretells the reestablishment of the Temple of Jerusalem, it must happen—"Prophecy demands it," according to Lindsey.[76] This notion is conjoined with "Providence," God's will as manifested on earth, something to a large extent (though not wholly, depending on theological perspective) preordained. Heavenly ordinances can manifest themselves through the light of goodness but also in shadows. Within a Christian framework this poses certain problems, raises certain tensions, including how to define the nature of satanic power, since the Devil's work must be (to avoid forms of theological dualism, or the equality of the powers of good and evil) sanctioned by God. Lindsey does not get into theological weeds, but he does have a strong sense of Satan's pervasive presence on earth. Satan continues to roam as the great deceiver, that same deceiver who tempted Eve but now presents himself in new forms to modern man by means of errant biblical scholarship and New Age spirituality. The way that this battle between good and evil plays out is not fully foreseeable in all its details, but Lindsey argues that God's ultimate victory is certain and that that moment will come under preordained circumstances clearly spelled out by scripture.

Lindsey dissolves any clear distinction between then (biblical times) and now. For example, to persuade readers that they must believe in the prophecies of scripture, he leans on the static qualities of human nature. He reminds readers of how Jews failed to understand Jesus as the Messiah for lack of interpretive acumen and consequently failed to see the truthfulness of prior prophetic pronouncements. After explaining this, he asks readers: "Will we repeat history? Will we fail to take the prophets literally and seriously?" Clearly, he hoped that his own prophetic voice would set things right, but that he had to publish his book at all reflects his sense that people continued to fail in their incredulity of prophetic figures, thus revealing an unchanging reality that can be altered only by the struggle of human will and the (timeless) workings of God.

For Lindsey's exegesis of scriptural prophecy to make sense, he must collapse modern and ancient categories. Lindsey's vision of the nearing Armageddon is largely sparked by the then relatively recent establishment of the State of Israel, which in itself presaged the biblically dictated reconstruction of the Jewish temple, its destruction, and its third (and final) reconstruction. But before this chain of events can occur, Lindsey argues that Israel will face turmoil and will have to confront a league of nations. Russia, as one might expect during the Cold War, is at the center of this. Of course, to make this claim, Lindsey grapples with the fact that scripture never mentions Russia. The specifics of this argument don't matter, but what does is the very fact that Lindsey feels comfortable collapsing a modern nation-state with what he considers an ethnic group from biblical times. Through tortured exegesis he can ascertain that the land of Magog mentioned in scripture refers to an actual ethnic group linked to a modern political grouping. To be able to make this argument, he has to ignore the vast gulf that exists between the biblical and the secular, indeed has to make a mockery of the passage of time and its worldly implications.

The end of secular time can be observed through the (again, preordained) repetition of history. The prophetic events as Lindsey sees them leading up to The End require the reestablishment of ancient institutions and beliefs. Prophecies decree spatial integrity as well; the new Jewish temple must be built over the original biblical structure. Only one problem. Lindsey points out that a holy Muslim space, the Dome of the Rock, rests over the temple's historical site. Ultimately and inevitably that would have to go, and with the new (old) temple, Judaism itself must be restored: "There will be a restitution to the Law of Moses with sacrifices and oblations in the general time of Christ's return."[77]

The Dylan of 1979–81 berated his audiences with incandescent "raps" that Clinton Heylin has rightly suggested were cribs of Lindsey's books. The content of these "Gospel Speeches" are important only insofar as they tell us about Dylan's engagement with Lindsey's thinking about time. In one of his most sulfurous talks, Dylan minces no words about the fact that he and his audiences were living "in the end times." He points to the imminent war in the Middle East as sign that Jesus is on his way back "to set his Kingdom in Jerusalem for a thousand years."[78] On another night, he got more specific, pointing to the violence soon to be unleashed on the Middle East by a northern power:

> Anyways, in the Bible it tells a specific thing in the Book of Revelations that just apply to these times, and it says that certain wars that soon—I can't say exactly when but soon anyway—so that at that time it mentions a country to the furthermost north, and has as its symbol the bear. And it's also spelt R-O-S-H in the Bible. This was written quite a few years ago. So it can't but be applied to one country that I know. But do you know another it can be applied to? Maybe you do. I don't know. Then there's another country called . . . can't remember what the name of it is but it's in the eastern part of the world, and it's got an army of two hundred million foot soldiers. Now there's only one country that that can actually be. So anyway, I was telling this story to these people. I shouldn't have been telling it to them. I just got carried away. I mentioned it to them and then I watched. And Russia was going to come down and attack the Middle East. It says this in the Bible.[79]

Because a rant in front of an audience expecting music is not the place to do it, Dylan did not go into all the evidence for his assertions, but we can safely assume that he was convinced by Lindsey's evidence that scripture spoke of lands and peoples that can be identified in modern circumstances, thus contracting the time and space between biblical antiquity and 1970s San Francisco.

In general, forces of good and evil dampen Dylan's sense of secular historical time. God's power is palpable in the everyday, in the good and especially in the bad. As he told fans at a show in San Francisco, "You know, we read in the newspaper every day what a horrible situation this world is in. Now God chooses to do these things in this world to confound the wise."[80] Dylan told another audience in San Francisco that he believed "the devil owns this world; he's called the God of this world."[81] Dylan's religion was (is?) an important filter for his historical understanding. His line of thinking required perceiving messages from the past about how the present and future will unfold through a reading of an ever-present divine will.

Scott Marshall has recently pointed out that when it comes to Dylan's spirituality, things are complicated, especially the interpenetration of Christian and Jewish influences. While we know that he had a "typical" Jewish upbringing, especially as evoked by Louie Kemp's recent book, it is not an identity that Dylan has promoted—much to the public chagrin of contemporaries such as Leonard Cohen and many lesser stars—except for a brief period *after* his tight embrace of Jesus in the late seventies and in the eighties.[82]

Ideologically, the transition, if indeed that's what we can call it, from Christianity back to Judaism was facilitated by important connective tissues, including a reverence for the Holy Land and its implications for now and the hereafter. Unsurprisingly, by the mideighties he had shown some interest in the Jewish Defense League, which propounded a hard-core Zionist and fierce anti-Arab sentiment under the controversial Brooklyn-born leader Meir Kahane, glibly called by some—intent on evoking biblical history—the "King of Israel." Kahane's form of Zionism depended, of course, on a spiritual and historical understanding of the covenant established between God and Jews and was thus dependent on Hebrew scripture and the notion of Jews as the chosen people, something further elaborated in secular history by a lachrymose past of violence, abuse, and marginalization. Kahane (and Lindsey for that matter) suggests that there needed to be a break with this cycle of oppression, and so he grounded his bilious and violent discourse under the banner of "Never Again," a reminder, as if it were needed, that extreme (and not extreme) forms of modern Zionism are inflected by a historicity born of the unfathomable murder experienced during the twentieth century.[83]

Dylan has not been consistent, but at least one of his tracks has embraced Kahane's brand of Zionism. The ironically titled "Neighborhood Bully," from *Infidels* (1983), a putatively "secular" album after his more or less Christian triptych of previous years, defends the State of Israel from many points of view, some of them historical. Strident and musically vacuous, it is nevertheless a loud response to Israel's critics by reminding the listener that Jews have always been at the receiving end of vitriol and violence, only to survive, presumably in light of God's will. Dylan underlines that Jews have overcome all their oppressors, from Egypt to Rome to Babylon. Tellingly, the song ends with a reflection on the interconnections between past, present, and future: asking first why Jews have suffered as they have and concluding that they stay, "running out the clock, time standing still." The remnants of past violence inform the present situation. In the past, just like today, suffering is the result not of sins committed but of an ordained reality that will be overcome by persistence.

The remembrance of Jewish suffering and oppressions undoubtedly affected Dylan's worldview. Recently resurfaced interviews with Tony Glover from 1971 reveal that though Dylan was apparently not victim of personal scorn, he was alive to anti-Semitism. During his first eighteen years he learned that "there were a lot of people that were prejudiced" and that "a lot of people are under the impression that Jews are just money lenders and merchants." Interestingly, Glover's typescript shows that "money lenders" has been added in Dylan's own hand to replace the typescript's "bankers," suggesting both an interest in exactitude and, just as importantly, an archaic sensibility that evoked medieval nomenclature. Dylan subsequently inserts a nuance that reveals deep historical engagement with the material origins of such stereotypes: "Well, they used to be [money lenders] cause that's all that was open to them. That's all they were allowed to do."[84]

The violence of anti-Semitism has unsurprisingly been important to Dylan. We hear, for example, of his wild enthusiasm for Isaac Bashevis Singer's historical novel *The Slave*, which chronicles the physical and spiritual torment of a mixed Christian and Jewish couple during times of persecution (sixteenth-century Poland), a story of immense literary power that is also an (imagined) historical reconstruction of a religiously violent and savage past.

Of course, most post-Biblical narratives of Jewish suffering pale in comparison to the horrors of Nazi Germany and its conquered lands. Such was the trauma of the Holocaust that the event has fundamentally reoriented our understandings of how to engage with the past, how nations cope with their dark histories, how, or even if, remembrance can and should be enacted, whether in so doing the ineffable horror of genocide is diminished. Moreover, and more broadly, the Holocaust has become a historical reference, almost a litmus test of other evils. Especially within the contexts of American and British culture, Nazism and its violence represent, according to the philosopher Susan Neiman, "the black hole in the heart of history, the apex of evil, the sin for which no expiation is possible, no condemnation sufficient."[85] There is absolutely no doubt that Dylan saw that darkness, especially as a Jew who was reaching adulthood right when awareness of Nazi-perpetrated genocide was becoming a baked-in feature of popular culture and discourse.[86]

If Britta Lee Shain, Dylan's one-time love interest, can be believed, in the eighties Dylan thought about writing a movie called *Nazi Whores*, "about Jewish women who escaped concentration camps": it would have been his most expansive, though not his most profound, treatment of Jews during the Third Reich.[87] Barring this (thankfully) film manqué, his comments on the Holocaust have been selective.

Though, or perhaps because, his thoughts on the Holocaust have not been made from an articulated Jewish viewpoint there is something methodical, cutting, and detached about his analysis. For example, in his spew of a long-form poem *Tarantula* (1966), we read this slap of a statement: "hitler [*sic*] did not change history. hitler WAS history."[88] This somewhat tortured phrase gets to the heart of Hitler's importance and the definitiveness of his actions as world-historical events and, as Seth Rogovy has pointed out, Dylan's embrace of a "great man" theory of history.[89] In the tripped-out pages of Dylan's book, the Holocaust was portrayed as a hinge moment, a moment of such magnitude that it usurps the past and provides a totalizing insight into time itself; perhaps the black hole Neiman evoked.

Dylan has deployed Nazi cruelty and its aftermath in finger-pointing songs. In "With God on Our Side" (1963), Dylan uses language of casual horror to tell us of how Jews had been fried in ovens. He says this to contrast those horrors with the forgiveness that followed World War II and the (partial) reinvitation of (West) Germany into a broader international community in the spirit of forgive and forget.

In his old age, Dylan's references to Nazi violence echo earlier aggressive defenses of the Jewish state. In *Chronicles* he claims that Ray Gooch (Dylan's creation) once asked him, "You ever heard of Auschwitz?" Dylan's response is a history lesson:

> Sure I had, who hadn't? It was one of the Nazi death camps in Europe and Adolf Eichmann, the chief Nazi Gestapo organizer who'd managed them, had been put on trial recently in Jerusalem . . . on the witness stand Eichmann declared he was merely following orders, but his prosecutors had no problem proving that he had carried out the mission with monstrous zeal and relish. . . . There was a lot of talk about sparing his life . . . but that would have been foolish. Even if he was set free he probably wouldn't last an hour. The State of Israel claimed the right to act as heir and executor of all who perished in the final solution. The trial reminds the whole world of what led to the formation of the Israeli state.[90]

Apart from revealing the fact that the memory of Nazi atrocities was front and center in his (and everyone's) mind in the sixties, Dylan underscores what he considers—undoubtedly too simplistically—the ligatures between obscene violence and the birth of Israel. In his opinion, it was Israel's charge to seek retribution and in that capacity to set the historical record straight, to show the evil of man as something real and horrifying and not the product of a corporative culture, of unwilling executioners.

The Eichmann trial was the product of a legal process organized by rules and norms, but there is a more visceral story to be told about Jews and Nazis. In 2012 Dylan alluded to some kind of mystico-biological sense of unforgetting. In comments that stirred some controversy—he was accused in an official lawsuit of stoking violence—Dylan claimed that just as Black people can sniff out a Klansman, and a Croat a Serb, "Jews can sense Nazi blood."[91] This might be a rhetorical infelicity or it might be an understanding of the ways in which the Holocaust marks all Jews, how they can intuit their enemies, and how blood possesses the past. Could this hold true for Dylan himself, right now and today? It doesn't really matter, except that his comment reveals something unquestionable: the extent to which the story of Jewish oppression and violence lurk in Dylan's conscious and subconscious and how this story is fundamentally an element of memory that through analysis and retelling becomes history.

Most religious traditions require forms of historical storytelling for the edification of believers or potential converts. The Bible itself was long seen (and is still seen) as the most important historical narrative until harder lines between the worldly and the spiritual were drawn when "science" became an alternate sphere of knowledge to the theological. But scripture has never been the only tool for spiritual growth and ecclesiastical consolidation—various forms of exegesis via sermons, songs, and other kinds of performance have provided the tools for teaching and understanding Biblical narratives and their significance. This topic is vast, so let's just touch on one activity, to the extent that Dylan has evoked it.

When Dylan accepted the 2017 MusiCares award, he delivered a long speech contextualizing and defending his work, and providing insights into what he deemed its roots. He mentioned individuals like

Johnny Cash and Joan Baez, and there were nods at folk and blues and traditional musical forms. Somewhat surprisingly, though, he also pointed listeners to the shadows of the Late Middle Ages and the Renaissance. He tied his work to the types of theatrical performances he says Shakespeare likely saw as a child: mystery plays. A reference so specific deserves contemplation. By making the connection, Dylan is placing his work within a tradition of Christian drama going back centuries, a form that was in fact dying off by the time Shakespeare witnessed it. These were events where scriptures came to life, where biblical stories were given a pulse, where the masses came close to the teachings of the church, and where biblicism met imagination. Surviving versions of mystery plays reenact, for example, the narrative of Noah's Ark, complete with edgy portrayals of Noah and his saucy wife exchanging barbs and innuendo.

For Dylan, there is a narratological link to this old tradition. He is deeply familiar with a genre of song that tell biblical tales. There are, to take examples at random, all those Christological songs that imagine the life of baby Jesus in John Jacobs Niles's 1958 album *I Wonder as I Wander*, an album Dylan would have known well. Or listen to Dylan on the *Basement Tapes* perform a blues-infused version of "Belshazzar," a song based on the Book of Daniel that tells the story "about a man / Who ruled Babylon and all its land / 'Round the city he built a wall / And declared that Babylon would never fall."

There is a performative link as well. Mystery plays are no longer "popular" in the way they were in the Middle Ages, but they survive in modern culture, especially among the devout. There is still a substantial tradition of biblical reenactments, some of which take violent forms, as in the well-known *senakulo* performance in the Philippines. Closer to home, fully staged productions of Christ's story with replicas of important biblical spaces are important attractions, especially along the Bible Belt. One of the biggest of these, in Eureka Springs, Arkansas, makes grandiose promises: "Staged in an outdoor amphitheater, the multi-level set, special lighting and sound effects, live animals, and a cast of 150 Biblically costumed actors come together to create the thrilling epic drama of Jesus Christ's last days on earth." Visitors are invited to "see the Easter story come to life."[92]

Dylan claims to have felt the frisson of participating in such spec-tacles. In *Chronicles* he thinks back to his first public performance, which supposedly occurred in the *Black Hills Passion Play of South Dakota*. This production, he says, came to town every year around Christmas, bringing actors and a quasimenagerie, including cages of chickens, a donkey, and a camel. He recalls that one year he played a Roman soldier as a nonspeaking extra, a humble thing that never-theless got him a spear, helmet, and breastplate. He felt like a star. "It felt like a tonic . . . as a Roman soldier I felt like part of everything, in the center of the planet, invincible."[93]

This sort of art is an extension of rituals that are fundamental to religious practices well-known to Dylan. Judeo-Christian tradi-tions invoke a biblical past by recalling and ritually performing con-crete events in a long religious narrative. Think of, for example, Yom Kippur, whose provenance goes back to the aftermath of Israelite exodus on Mount Sinai as described in the Hebrew scriptures, or to the various rituals by which Christians perform the Last Supper as described in the New Testament. These are spiritually charged forms of commemoration and devotion, brought to life by historical reenactment. In some instances—take the sacrament of the Eucha-rist in Catholic tradition—there is an actual collapse of time, as the performance of the Last Supper, the sharing of the body and blood of Christ, is not symbolic but real by means of transubstantiation.

The performative aspect of Dylan's religious life is, save for a handful of years, opaque. Indeed, as far as I can tell, only once out-side of a concert venue has personal devotion become truly public: his second and much-publicized visit to the Western Wall in Jerusa-lem (1983). There he was observed davening, taking part in a gestural tradition of stylized prayer going back to antiquity. We can't know what Dylan felt, but in theory, prayer would have been enhanced by his presence at a spiritually exalted site, the place where God chose to dwell in Davidic times. Dylan's encounter with such a holy place allowed him to "touch" history, to feel its nourishing energies and, perhaps, from a certain point of view, contemplate a future return, as discussed earlier, of an ancient structure in modern times.

The point here is twofold. On the one hand, spiritual and religious traditions require us to think about how they are historical activities, even when the limits of history are pushed to extremes. On the other hand, religious traditions (and certainly the ones that Dylan subscribes to) have performative aspects that represent the past and can even bring the past to life. These are not activities that we would usually call "historical practices" because they belong to another "disciplinary" or ontological realm, and yet they are nevertheless acts of historical recreation and must be taken into account as part of the historical matrix that informs our subject.

GHOST ELECTRICITY

Muff Winwood, who was at the time part of the Spencer Davis Group, claims that when Dylan went to Birmingham (England) in 1966, he talked and talked about "how he was into ghosts and he loved Britain because of the history and everything and he thought there'd be some wonderful ghosts around." Someone told him there was a big abandoned mansion in Worcestershire where the ghosts of a man and his dog wandered around the property. A specter-hungry Dylan insisted on going in the wee hours after a concert. When they got there, amid the moonglow and the ivy of a misty sculptured garden, the entourage stopped to listen . . . and they heard a dog bark. Winwood remembers Dylan being "convinced that he's heard the ghost of the dog! He was like a kid!" Three years later Dylan would still be talking about that night when he "went out to see a haunted house, where a man and his dog was supposed to have burned in the thirteenth century. Boy, that place was spooky."[94]

Although Dylan hasn't spoken extensively on the topic, there's no doubt he sees ghosts, mostly metaphorical ones, but maybe not. Larry Charles (cowriter of *Masked and Anonymous*) recalls having met with Dylan after he'd visited a Civil War cemetery and realizing that "the bleakness and the sadness and the poetry of it was really moving to him."[95] Charles's observation is supported by Dylan himself, who told Bill Flanagan in 2009 that the American South is "filled with rambling ghosts and disturbed spirits. . . . There are war fields everywhere . . . a lot of times even in people's backyards. . . . I felt the ghosts from the bloody battle that Sherman fought against Forrest and drove him out. There's an eeriness to the town. A sadness that lingers. Elvis must have felt it too."[96]

It is easy enough to dismiss this kind of talk as wacky, weird, just poetic, just another rhetorical flourish. But to do so would be to continue the secularist, objectivist, scientific biases of modern scholarship that only haltingly and unwillingly take seriously forms of the supernatural or its kin. Murray Leeder, for example, has written an absorbing article on ghosts in Dylan's oeuvre (and in *Masked & Anonymous* in particular) but stops (mostly) where the tropes do. To emphasize the literary qualities of Dylan's spookier evocations, however, might undermine the importance of ghosts and, more broadly, the supernatural to the American psyche. Indeed, if we think back to the nineteenth century—to pick a period often on Dylan's mind—we have to consider the Spiritualist movement defined by the actual communication with the hereafter and even its visual manifestations by means of modern technology—photography—where the dead were said (and seen) to appear. This photo-spiritual practice was embraced, especially after the carnage of the Civil War, by many, including Abraham Lincoln's widowed wife. Dylan must know about all this given his Civil War interests, but the example is important for our present purpose because recent scholarship has reminded us that such activities are constitutive of American history and are marked by a very real historicity. Historian Molly McGarry urges us to accept as valid "a historical moment in which communing with the dead offered the potential for affective communication across time, personal transformations, and utopian political change." The practices of séance, the public communications about these otherworldly connections, and the various forms of evidence used to legitimate these connections were forms of affective historical engagement replete with embedded messages and information about potential futures.[97]

There is no doubt that apart from evoking ghosts by means of literary practice, more concrete searches for spirits color Dylan's engagement with music. For example, we hear of him taking a tour—a public tour at that—to John Lennon's childhood home in Liverpool, and of him wandering off in the rain looking for Bruce Springsteen's house (and being arrested along the way).[98] When he went to Neil Young's childhood home in Winnipeg, Canada, the current residents took him up to Young's old room and Dylan mused, "OK, so this was his view, and this was where he listened to his music."[99] We can't know for certain what Dylan was looking for, but at the very least we can assume that he was after some connectivity with the past, perhaps even a sense that he could for a moment come close to seeing things through the eyes of a Young or a Lennon. In this, Dylan would conform to old practices—such as the pilgrimage—by which Christians visited sites associated with saints to absorb some of their spiritual electricity.

Admittedly, this kind of experience need not be spiritual at all. As geographers have noted, there is a strong sense among many that presence in a place can lead to the absorption of its energy. Richard Lang has argued that, for example, "Inhabiting is an act of incorporation; it is a situation of active, essential acquisition . . . embracing and assimilating a certain sphere of foreign reality to its own body. In this sense, incorporation is essentially the movement from the strange to the familiar."[100] Such a sense of incorporation is predicated on an existing reality constituted by the accumulated stories of a place, and in this way, I would suggest, such experiences are historical ones.

Perhaps Dylan's most famous—certainly his most publicized—communion with the dead occurred with Allen Ginsberg at his side when they visited Jack Kerouac's grave in Lowell, Massachusetts. There, they sat reading his poetry and presumably somehow convening with his ghost. To be sure, their gesture (and the photo op) can be analyzed in the realm of the symbolic and the commemorative, but we can think of it as a practice with supernatural overtones as well. Think of Robert Johnson, one of Dylan's great influences. As the story goes, when Johnson was learning his craft, before a famed encounter at a crossroads (which Dylan also claims to have had), he was taught (at least in part) in a graveyard in Mississippi by another talented Black guitarist, Ike Zimmerman (yes, Zimmerman). According to Johnson's most indefatigable biographers, Bruce Conforth and Gayle Dean Wardlow, Zimmerman drew on hoodoo traditions in his belief that "the only place. . . . you could really learn to play the blues, was in a cemetery at night."[101]

Dylan would certainly understand this because he dwells in the land of ghosts: "You're talking to a person that feels like he's walking around in the ruins of Pompeii." Or, as he put it in "Rollin' and Tumblin'," "The night's filled with shadows, the years are filled with early doom / I've been conjuring up all these dead souls from these crumblin' tombs."

When Mikal Gilmore interviewed Dylan for *Rolling Stone* in 2012, he probably didn't see it coming. At one point Dylan excitedly showed him a beat-up copy of *Hell's Angel: The Life and Times of Sonny Barger and the Hell's Angels Motorcycle Club* by Sonny Barger and Keith Zimmerman. He then had Gilmore read into his tape recorder a snippet of text describing how in 1964 an early Hells Angel president, Bobby Zimmerman, was killed in a motorcycle accident. Dylan pointed out the excerpt to show that he (born Robert Zimmerman) had been "transfigured." Gilmore, confused and perplexed, seeks clarification. Did Dylan mean he had been transformed or is he talking about transmigration, the passing of a soul into a different body? Nope. Dylan continues with studied opacity: "You can go and learn about it from the Catholic Church, you can learn about it in some old mystical books, but it's a real concept. It's happened throughout the ages. Nobody knows who it's happened to, or why. But you get real proof of it here and there. It's not like something you can dream up and think. It's not like conjuring up a reality or like reincarnation—or like when you might think you're somebody from the past but have no proof." He emphasizes that the idea doesn't have "anything to do with the past or the future." He continues, "So when you ask some of your questions, you're asking them to a person who's long dead. You're asking them to a person that doesn't exist." This before concluding,

"Transfiguration is what allows you to crawl out from under the chaos and fly above it. That's how I can still do what I do and write the songs I sing and just keep on moving."[102]

What on earth does this mean? On the one hand, it's tempting to shrug it all off as typical Dylan bullshit, the momentary return of a sharp-clawed cat playing with his journalistic prey. But, clearly, Dylan has been thinking about his relationship to the other Bobby for a while. He mentions the episode (though not transfiguration) in *Chronicles*, in a discussion about his name change to Bob Dylan. In something close to a non sequitur, after a discussion of how he landed on his new name, he concludes by telling the reader about the Hells Angel: "As far as Bobby Zimmerman, I'm going to give this to you right and straight and you can check it out." He recounts Bobby's death: "That person is gone. That was the end of him."[103] In this thudding conclusion, Dylan seems to suggest the entwinement of his identity with someone else's, both of whom ended, even if the current Dylan had another life left in him.

Although Dylan told Gilmore that his experience had nothing to do with time, in almost the same breath, he changes his tune: "I had a motorcycle accident in 1966. I already explained to you about new and old. Right? Now, you can put this together any way you want." Clearly, he pinpoints whatever experience he had within a defined chronology and, what's more, he connects it to previous comments in the same interview in which he talked about how time overlapped, how the fifties of his youth were not over until the midsixties of his adulthood. Are we to extrapolate from this that the old Bobby and the new Bobby overlapped and were subject to some mutually enhancing changes?

It's not worth going down this rabbit hole, but it is worth pointing out that Dylan is espousing a version of time that is, again, as discussed above, not earthly, and in which the typical divisions of past, present, and future collapse. In biblical terms, transfiguration is that moment before Christ entered Jerusalem, high atop what extrabiblical interpretation has suggested was Mount Tabor, with Peter, James, and John. While there, Jesus's appearance changed, and he emanated light, and the voice of God was heard confirming that Jesus was His son. Within the Catholic tradition—which Dylan mentions—it can be understood, as Pope Benedict XVI suggested, as the "full manifestation of God's light."[104] It is the moment, as the Catholic catechism says, when Jesus disclosed "his divine glory."[105] The moment thus unites the secular (Christ's mortal body) with the eternal (God). If we take this into account, and squint a little, we can see that Dylan might be referring to a process by which the temporal—of this earth and time—interacts with the spiritual, something fundamentally timeless.

The effects of this timeless event manifest themselves in worldly revelation. As Andrew McCarren has plausibly suggested, Dylan's concept of transfiguration led to a heightened state of awareness. In trying to explain transfiguration, Dylan tells Gilmore that it leads to something many people never experience because "some people never really develop into who they're supposed to be. They get cut off. They go off another way. It happens a lot. We all see people that that's happened to. We see them on the street. It's like they have a sign hanging on them." Together with other statements Dylan has made in the past, McCarren concludes that Dylan understands the phenomenon "involved developing into the person that you're destined to become—and by doing so, actualizing the evolving picture you have in your mind of who you are and what you're about."[106]

What Dylan believes here is less important than the fact that a set of (spiritual) beliefs allows him to conceptualize the possible connection among divided bodies and souls.

This notion has musical equivalents.

Dylan has claimed that his songs were "not written with the idea in mind that anyone else would sing them." They were meant for him to perform. Others might cover the song, but "it can't be expected that a performer get under the song, inside and blow it out. It's like getting inside of another person's soul." Jimi Hendrix was the exception. "He sang them [Dylan's songs] exactly the way they were intended to be sung & played them the same way. he did them the way I wouldve done them if I was him. never thought much about it at the time but now that the years have gone by, i see that the message must have been his message thru & thru . . . i realize he mustve felt it pretty deeply inside & out & that somewhere back there, his soul & my soul were on the same desert."[107] Here we have the language of a mystical union where the truth of a song can transcend individuals and time, and where that truth can be uttered in unison even if temporally apart.

This resonates in interesting ways with how Dylan has talked about forms of inspiration. Most famously, in his "Best Album" acceptance speech at the 1998 Grammys he implies a mystical connection with another rock legend: "When I was sixteen or seventeen years old, I went to see Buddy Holly play at Duluth National Guard Armory and I was three feet away from him . . . and he *looked* at me. And I just have some sort of feeling that he was—I don't know how or why—but I know he was with us all the time we were making this record in some kind of way."[108] Again, reading too much into this is dangerous and yet, whether Dylan believes it or not, it's important that in framing his creative process as a connective experience with the dead, he is reaching for a trope about (quite likely a belief in) the possibility of souls being disrespectful of secular time and its limitations.

MUSIC IN TIME

Music making is a profoundly historical activity. Psychologists—not to mention experience—have long noted the ability of music to evoke memories. Indeed, studies increasingly show the connection of listening to music with feelings of nostalgia. Aspects of musical experience also provide lasting impressions, most obviously in the form of earworms that fix an aural "image" in our brains and functions much like an involuntary memory—the snatches of music you cannot get out of your head. Moreover, the experience of music, its very apprehension, requires the listener to use their memory to anticipate what comes next, and in doing so, if we want to get philosophical about it, they must bring together past, present, and future.[109]

These fundamental qualities in music allow it to evoke (or appear to evoke) a specific past, your own or an imagined one. Classical singer Ian Bostridge, in a discussion of Franz Schubert's nineteenth-century song cycle *Die Winterreise* (The Winter's Journey), dwells on the "sense we have about music, about its ability to summon up, to encapsulate the moods and subjectivities of past times, whether in our histories as individuals or those of other cultures."[110] The realm of classical music is a site of activity beholden to historical reconstruction either through the oft-pronounced veneration of the composer's intentions or in sometimes militant historicist practices such as the historically informed performance movement that once took early music by storm with an emphasis on replicating through style and period instruments the sound and feel of pre-Romantic music as it "really" was. Critics of this movement point out that such antiquarian pursuits push against the organic process of music making that defines the classical tradition and so this imitative impulse is little more than a marker of modern inclinations, not historical accuracy.[111]

Such debates are central to wrangles about folk music. Although, as Robert Cantwell argues, folk is all deeply rooted in social unrest, its form and function have been a source of contention.[112] The cult of purity and authenticity (with strong imitative elements) often seemed at odds with a folk movement more interested in commenting on and inserting itself into current events and popular plights. Efforts to unite the two streams of folk activity occasionally led to contortions, such as the editorial comment in the first edition of *Broadside*, a publication focused on "topical songs": "BROADSIDE may never publish a song that could be called a 'folk song.' But let us remember that many of our best folk songs were topical songs at their inception."[113]

In a sense, these ambiguities, these different paths, are iterations of changing sensibilities at the very start of the folk movement. Matthew Gelbart has shown that in the late eighteenth and early nineteenth centuries there was a shift from understanding music of the folk as artifacts, time capsules, objects to be gazed at to understand the nation in its purest forms, to something much more (historically) expansive—a tradition that "could rise above being a mere tool for use in discovering the past, itself coming to reify a shared cultural history, as a living bridge from past to present."[114]

There are many techniques to "capture" that elision of past and present. It is striking, for example, that a person like Alan Lomax, in his quest to find and reproduce (via recordings) the (musical) origins of America, went to prisons in hopes of finding the songs and singers least tainted by modernity, "where," as he said, "Negroes are almost entirely isolated from whites, dependent upon the resources of their own group for amusement."[115] Segregated and in cages, then, Black singers were to perform and reveal the origins of a certain kind of American song, the closest we can get to an ur- form.[116]

These sorts of folk authenticities are not only performed but are also learned. This is particularly true among those who have favored an aesthetic route to folk music over a more overtly political one, a type of folkie evoked by Izzie Young in 1959 when he exclaimed, "Long live Perry Lederman for raptly listening to Blind Blake's recordings and forcing everyone to hear his attempts at recreating his guitar technique!"[117] People like Lederman were not satisfied with drawing influence from past traditions but wanted to reproduce older styles. Dylan, of course, would be among those who would listen, learn, copy, and perform.

Confidence in re-creating a musical past does not, of course, ensure the accuracy of those re-creations; scholarship in many fields has rendered hollow any and all claims to "authenticity," but it is the imagined accuracy that matters. Richard Sonn, a historian at the University of Arkansas, has an interesting story to tell along these lines. Sonn has been known to hang around battlegrounds in period appropriate garb with a fiddle in hand. More than once, a tourist or onlooker has asked him to play a typical Civil War song, maybe that doleful tune that accompanied Ken Burns's legendary documentary *The Civil War*. There's only one problem, Sonn points out with a little bit of a grin: the "Ashokan Farewell" is a melody based on a Scottish tune repurposed toward the end of the twentieth century by a musician from the Bronx, Jay Ungar.[118]

Dylan was, of course, drawn in by this semblance of antiquity. Among his influences, Dylan points to John Jacob Niles, a composer, collector, and performer of folk songs. He remembers him appearing like "an old scary woman out of a Shakespeare play, with a high piercing eerie wailing voice . . . he had white hair, long white hair, and he played a strange instrument that I don't think anyone had ever seen, something that maybe came from the old country and they didn't have many of them."[119] This appreciation of Niles touches on several tropes of the folk tradition (especially of Dylan's youth): the Shakespearean connection, a touch of the gothic, and a heavy accretion of dust.

The power of music is, at least in part, its ability to simulate "reality" using means that are foreign to everyday life. We don't go around singing to friends, colleagues, and family; the singer or musician is not in the game of representing nature (save for the occasional evocation of particular natural sounds like a bird's song or a creaking door), music does not possess or enshrine mimetic qualities as typically defined. But what if we look at "mimesis"—the representation of reality—from a slanted perspective? Stephen Halliwell has suggested that in its earliest ancient Greek forms, the term was probably linked to musical performance and would not have had the necessary or exclusive connotation of "simulation" but instead would have referred to a persuasive style based on performative and rhetorical tools judged by the impressiveness of representations "in terms of their success in drawing the hearer or viewer into a strong engagement with the possibilities of experience they depict."[120] Mimesis, according to Halliwell, is a multifaceted and contested aesthetic category, but this particular affective strand is valuable to us, as it raises the possibility that music is a tool for a particular kind of seductive and convincing experience that can, in some circumstances, intimate reality or, just as importantly, suspend everything and create a sensory experience that includes and surpasses reality. In either case, this is a theoretical way to get at a commonsense feeling among music listeners: it's the thing about music that makes us cry when we hear a chord.

Music thus has something of an incantatory quality that appears to evoke a particularly powerful truth. To take an important example, in the aftermath of the Holocaust, music was one among many artistic means of dealing with, thinking about, and even evoking past horrors. As with representations of the Holocaust in general, there are debates about the extent to which such activities are morally responsible given the enormity of the event. The problem is redoubled when artistic representations do not stay within parameters of truth and accuracy. In the musical realm, some of the most incisive attempts to deal with the memory of Jewish slaughter have aimed not to reproduce a facsimile of the past but to evoke a believable, emotive past. Take, for example, Arnold Schoenberg's *A Survivor from Warsaw*, a cantata that tells the story of an imagined concentration camp survivor. The piece does not tell a "true" story but a story that might have been true and that, in any case, can convince the auditor (by means of various modernist techniques) of the story's vitality.

We can think of a similar dynamic closer to home, as these issues of historical representation have taken a front seat in popular culture thanks to incredibly popular works such as Lin-Manuel Miranda's *Hamilton*. In the case of *Hamilton*, we are dealing with a narrative that claims truthfulness and is based on Ron Chernow's biography of the founding father. It is "straight" history by musical means, even if its many elements (multiracial cast, hip-hop-inflected music) have nothing to do with the period being represented.

This musico-historical genre, if one might call it that, is crucial to the folk tradition. It might suffice to remember that during the nineteenth century, a general fascination with Napoleon Bonaparte (a figure that appears in Dylan's work more than once) translated into songs about him and his exploits. This to the extent that, according to Stephen Wade, "no homegrown military figure, neither Washington nor Lee, Jackson nor Grant has been commemorated so widely in American folk music."[121] We hear such titles as "Napoleon Crossing the Rhine" and "Bonaparte's Retreat from Moscow," "The Battle of Waterloo," and "The Battle of the Nile." A famous anecdote goes that one Uncle John, a fiddler in Pine Bluff, Kentucky, once performed a tune titled "Napoleon Crossing the Rockies" for a scholar. The professor thought he should share the fact that Napoleon had never done such a thing. Uncle John skipped a beat and answered, "Well, historians differ." The story, true or not, takes us where we want to go, to the intersection of tradition, songstering, and the (ambiguities) of historical production by means of music and performance.

Dylan has expressed aspects of music's potential verisimilitude. He has said that "in songs, you have to tell people about something they didn't see and weren't there for, and you have to do it as if you were."[122] He has also said that for a song to be effective, the singer needs to have experienced that thing, to truly know what it's about. Given these strands, perhaps we have been thinking about Dylan's performance "theory" in terms that are too pedestrian: what if the so-called masks worn by Dylan are not mere costumes? What if, in fact, these masks can be something more akin to embodiments? If these notions are tenable, they suggest a musical realm where time and space can meld, where we can establish realms of possibility for the intrusion of the past in the present and its futuricity too. This might require the suspension of disbelief. It also requires a set of activities, a set of practices, that enable the viewer to take a ride into some version of the past, into history. We'll deal with this in due time.

CONCLUSION

I hope that the reader has arrived at this resting spot somewhat disoriented, perhaps a little dissatisfied, or, better yet, wanting more. This has been a quick tour of many historical activities, many historical vistas, that can safely be said to have influenced Dylan throughout his (professional) life. By taking this kaleidoscope view, I don't mean to suggest that all of these historical vistas equally or consistently exist within Dylan's mind as organizing principles or models for what I will suggest in later chapters were his own historical practices. The point here has been to suggest a range of historical enterprises that potentially provided Dylan with a historical tool kit that he could use, abuse, or ignore over time. If, as Sean Wilentz has suggested, Dylan provides insights into a historical consciousness, this chapter has tried to describe some coordinates of Dylan's own.[123]

CHAPTER 2

"Conjuring Up All These Long Dead Souls"

How Dylan "Does" History

So far, I've focused on the imaginary and have tried to establish some forms of Dylan's historical thinking. This chapter pivots to action by delving into how Dylan produces historically evocative work. I'll suggest the techniques that Dylan uses to re-present and re-create the past (and pastness) before live (and imagined) audiences.

BITS AND PIECES

If Dylan once attributed his output to some form of miraculous inspiration, if he could dash off a song in ten minutes and on the back of a cocktail napkin, we know that certain practices have also aided in the process. Put simply: it's all in the scraps. Larry Charles, whom we've met as the director and cowriter of *Masked and Anonymous*, got a glimpse of the magic while visiting Dylan's office in Santa Monica: "He brings out this very ornate beautiful box, like a sorcerer would, and he opens the box and dumps all these pieces of scrap paper on the table . . . and yes, that is exactly what he does . . . every piece of scrap paper was a hotel stationary, little scraps from Norway and from Belgium and Brazil and places like that, and each little piece of paper had a line, like some kind of little line scribbled or a name scribbled . . ."[1] Future scholars, with the benefit of the Bob Dylan

Archive in Tulsa, will be able to delve the depths of his approach, as there is hotel stationary aplenty there. For our purposes, the activity itself matters more than what it has produced.

Broadly, Dylan's technique concretizes the "folk process." At least in its most pristine formulation this process refers to an *oral* tradition that undergoes editing, borrowing, and rearrangement to produce cultural materials representative not so much of individual performers but of a *volkgeist*. In the postwar version of folk revivalism, part of the movement cringed and kvetched about the challenges posed by the demons of commercialization and cults of personality. To purists, every time a soulless clog signed up with Columbia Records (as Dylan did in 1962), the possibility of authentic folk music was diminished. You might sing folk material, but the process itself was twisted, mangled, and divorced from its most democratic elements.[2]

The stitching together of materials is not a product of folk sensibilities alone. Indeed, it is a marker of (popular) culture writ large. Richard Middleton refers to the soldering of different, often disparate musical and textual materials as "articulations." Steven Rings further explains that such a dynamic "refers not only to the combination of disparate cultural elements, but also to the ways in which the resultant structures generate emergent, often unpredictable new meanings."[3] Musical culture, and not just that of the *volk* in any pristine sense, results from reconfiguring traditional or extant raw materials to (seemingly) new ends.

Dylan's conjoining of materials and the transformational role played by the authorial figure in that process also fits neatly into the story of modernist art. Thomas Crow has argued that "folk authenticity" was a "constituent part of the belief system that established a viable avant-garde for the visual arts of America."[4] Such authenticities were in part established by artists collecting cultural and material flotsam and jetsam to evoke a sense of the past.[5] In this spirit, one might look at Jasper Johns's *Flag*—a mixed-media depiction of the American flag—which Crow describes as "a short list of components ordered by the most rudimentary of formulae" intending to produce meaning based on the engagement of the viewer with a universally apprehensible icon.[6]

Dylan has explored the theme of recombination and re-creation at length in his pictorial work. He did this most explicitly when he dipped his toes into "revisionist art." He took existing mass media scraps—magazines—and reshuffled them to (mostly) ironic or comedic effects.[7] In his paintings, too, where the method of borrowing and appropriation is not as clear and up-front, he has been a promiscuous borrower. For example, works from his *Asia Series* were clearly based on and sometimes directly copied from old photographs, despite press kit claims that Dylan "often draws and paints while on tour, and his motifs bear corresponding impressions of different environments and people."[8]

Dylan has always been in tune with different literary approaches emphasizing promiscuity. For example, he deeply admired William Burroughs, who experimented with cut-up techniques: taking existing texts, tearing them apart, and putting them back together. Dylan told interviewers in the sixties that he was exploring methods along those lines. In an outtake from *Dont Look Back* we hear Dylan talking with a slur, swallowed by the mist of fatigue and who knows what else, describing a method by which he writes a song, cuts it up, and reconstitutes it.[9] He takes a sheet of paper, folds and tears it, to demonstrate. If indeed this is what he did in those days—and Dylan's description is so halting that it is hard to tell—he is describing an approach that comes from the interiority of the artist and not from a historical or external warehouse of texts. This would make sense with regard to the Dylan of the times as he moved away from plain folk music and its historical fetters. What matters is that Dylan was experimenting with formal—as opposed to "organic," traditional—fragmentation and reconstitution at the start of his career.

More than Burroughs, Dylan was crucially influenced by T. S. Eliot's *The Wasteland,* and implicitly by its ideological underpinnings. In a famous (polemical) essay on the role of tradition in poetry, Eliot writes that "the poet's mind is in fact a receptacle for seizing and storing up numberless feelings, phrases, images, which remain there until all particles can be united to form a new compound are present together."[10] This magpie quality is the result of what Eliot deems essential to the poet: a "historical sense," which he defines as "a perception, not only of the pastness of the past, but of its presence."[11] In such a formulation—and this is important—it would seem that the very act of writing poetry (or music) is a historical enterprise, an act of historical reproduction, an invocation of preceding cultural stuff.

If Eliot spoke about poetry, (academic) history proper—in terms of technique and sense—is not much different. We can glance back all the way to the Renaissance revival of classical culture that inspired a renewed interest in ways of writing and reading history. In those days—say, Italy in the fifteenth and sixteenth centuries—readers were taught to excerpt and copy juicy bits of historical narratives into commonplace books for future use in historical writing or other rhetorical activities. Thus, historians were (and are) beholden, by necessity, to cut-and-paste methods. To be sure, history cannot be (should not be) assembled at random, but it is the fruit of locating variegated sources to create a story or coherent argument. Whether we are writing about the past descriptively or analytically, we need to cull bits and pieces of old things (and new)—quotes and ideas—from a range of raw materials that are subsequently packaged in a way that suits authorial needs.

Dylan, especially but by no means exclusively late Dylan, is an inveterate poacher of the antique. The long list of borrowings presumably gathered by cut-and-paste methods mentioned above would be too exhaustive and is rather well known by now anyway. One example will suffice. "High Water (For Charley Patton)" from *"Love and Theft"* (2001) is a masterclass in restitching disparate cultural materials to newish ends. From the song's very title, Dylan is gesturing pointedly at Patton's "High Water Everywhere" (1929). Aside from Patton himself, whose "Shake It, Break It" is also referenced in the song, Dylan "steals" from Robert Johnson's "Dust my Broom"; a traditional song, "The Cuckoo Bird"; Thomas Hood's poem "The Wise Little Pig"; and scripture too. The song also brings together a series of historical figures: aside from Patton, we have the likes of Charles Darwin, Bertha Mason, Big Joe Turner, and George Lewis, all of whom are repurposed within the logic of the song, a logic that is profoundly historical, in its evocation of the Mississippi's periodic flooding going back at least to the great flood of 1927, and later floods as well.

But borrowings, even of ancient things, do not necessarily mean that any given song is profoundly historical. You could take an old line, an old name, to sing a song about a very modern topic that breaks to pieces any sense of pastness. But Dylan *does* sometimes create historical artifacts both by borrowing at will, often aggressively so, *and* by ensuring that the final package—the song—is confected to maintain a sense that it comes from a different time and place.

Historians avoid anachronisms, and Bob Dylan kind of does too. One of the things that (more or less) distinguishes the historiographical tradition of the Renaissance (to which we owe a lot) from what came before is an expanded conception of the difference between then and now. In medieval times, it was not uncommon to represent ancient Romans in contemporary medieval garb. However, since the fourteenth, fifteenth, and sixteenth centuries, historians have *tried* (though often failed) to represent the past on its own terms. As a result, today we can hardly take seriously any *historical* representation of the deep past that incorporates modern elements—think of a scene of soldiers during the French Revolution or the American Civil War riding tanks. The distinctiveness of past and present can be and is often diminished by various time-bending routines, experiences, and assumptions, but even the full understanding of chronological flexibility requires (at least in Western culture) a sense of *difference*. For example, the notion of timelessness is dependent on a sense that then and now are two different things that can be in fact or imaginatively smushed together.

There is a tension between historical integrity and historical illusion in Dylan's songs. In his work, material by a twentieth-century author can meld with that of a nineteenth-century Southern poet or an ancient Greek chronicler. But even in moments such as these, disparate fragments are often brought together in such a way as to elide the historical distance of his sources. Thus, even though there might be internal anachronisms within a song or album, the effect is historicizing. If Charles Darwin and Big Joe Turner do not belong together (temporally) as they appear in "High Water," the song, and indeed the record to which it belongs, *"Love and Theft,"* does not at any point suggest anything having to do with the fin de siècle or the newish millennium that produced it. In fact, the whole album has nothing to suggest a plausible present setting at all, save maybe for three or four car references and, if you want to stretch it, now-arcane technologies such as the radio.

The trick to creating a sense of historicity in Dylan's work depends on forcing the listener to take an imaginative leap. The viewer/listener cannot feel that they are experiencing something current or readily apprehensible. For the song to work historically, Dylan needs to create a temporal distance.

The means by which he does this are many. Part of it is linguistic: clever or just bizarre linguistic turns such as the use of "fare-thee-well," "morn," "fine and fair," or peculiar constructions such as "come away from my window," or epithets like "dirty rotten scoundrel" and "feisty wench." At other times he evokes old technologies like the horse and buggy, old dances like the jitterbug, long-play records, etcetera. His songs are also populated by people long gone: Napoleon and old Roman kings, not to mention Abraham and assorted saints.

Ultimately, music itself is the great evoker of various pasts. If the language and imagery in Dylan's songs can cause minor or major forms of alienation, melodies and musical gestures function as primary distancing *and* seductive devices. From the very start of Dylan's career, nestled in the bosom urban folkies, he drew on tunes that were expected to have a Celtic, Appalachian, or Delta hue. Dylan is no longer passing a basket around, nor is he part of the folk scene proper, but his music of the past twenty years is thick with dust and rust deviating vastly from the common fare in music with mass appeal. Take, for example, Dylan's very close borrowing of Muddy Waters's "Rollin' and Tumblin'" for his own song by that same name, or his equally aggressive lift from Bobby Fuller's "New Shade of Blue" in his love song/murder ballad "Soon After Midnight." The listener does not need to know the precise nature of the borrowing or the borrowing at all, all they have to do is listen to know that what is being served is not of modern vintage. Audiences in general recognize that these new songs are, in form and function, arcane—they take you back even if you don't know where. Importantly, this is not the function of Dylan being old. Paul McCartney and Mick Jagger are just as old but they arrive at different musical conclusions. Their new and old material has a lot of baggage—their personal histories inflect how audiences relate to them—but their songs are not meant to suggest a pastness.

If Mick Jagger today is doing a pretty good imitation of Mick Jagger back then, Dylan is going out of his way to avoid self-repetition. As Andrea Cossu and Lee Marshall suggest, he works hard to create new authenticities at odds with his own past.[12] Dylan is trying to ensure that he's not there, and in doing so helps render possible the apprehension of his songs minus their modern trappings.[13]

We might think about Dylan's absence through the lens of objectivity. Although many, though not all, academic historians, jaded as we are, might cringe at the concept, this nineteenth-century holdover still influences how we think about various nonfiction genres. Thus, in American culture (and less so in Europe and many other cultures), journalists and their institutions feel compelled to hide ideological sensibilities and, even in the most patently untrue cases, claim to be "fair and balanced." Historians are also supposed to be "unbiased" and removed from the objects of their research; they are, to the extent possible, supposed to suppress the self to represent the past accurately. The historian, like the nineteenth-century ideal of a scientist, can be imagined as an observational vessel, a conduit for truth. In popular culture, if historians are thought of having any scientific value at all, it is not because they are a part of *interpretive* communities but because they belong to a guild of fact churners.

Since Dylan is a song writer, a person given to the gods of art rather than science, it might seem far-fetched to suggest he maintains a level of objectivity. And yet . . . There are two intermingled suppositions articulated by Dylan that place him within an objectivist camp. Dylan has said that his art is a sort of truth, maybe even a higher truth, and so, at least occasionally, performer and audience connive to experience the (re)presentation of "reality." Importantly, this is accomplished through a process of disengagement in which the author is disentwined from what he produces. Put simply, finding the "real" Dylan, the individual, in his artistic output is almost impossible, and this is by design.

This needs to be underlined because there is a compulsive temptation to see the personal embedded in anything an artist does. In the post-Romantic age when art and individual genius are so tightly bound, even brilliant scholars have (errantly) tried to piece together the lives of artists such as Shakespeare, who have left only scrappy evidence of their private lives, through a close reading of their oeuvre. With distant figures, the excuse for such an approach might be the scarcity of other sources, but that is certainly not the case with Dylan. Perhaps because Dylan has cultivated a kind of privacy unheard of in modern pop culture, perhaps because his songs are deemed to be so heavy, the connection between song and self seem irresistible. As a result, Paul Williams could, in a manner I wholeheartedly reject, claim that a necessary precept for understanding Dylan is the idea that performers, "however much they may try to hide in their private lives, always give themselves away at the moment they perform before an audience."[14]

Dylan has long understood and hated this tic. In a recently unearthed interview, he expresses his frustration sharply and hyperbolically (and funnily) by asking why songs by other artists aren't used for autobiographical purposes: "Do you think Johnny Cash shot a man in Reno? . . . Or that Paul Simon would throw himself down over a troubled Hudson River and let somebody use him as a bridge?"[15]

Frustration must have been (and surely continues to be) that much more acute because of the extent to which Dylan has, with lapses here and there, rejected the autobiographical and the personal in his work. Apart from "Ballad in Plain D" (1964) and "Sara" (1976)—these are both glaring and (from where I sit) unfortunate exceptions—there are no songs that conform fully to the outlines of Dylan's biography as we know it, giving Dylan plenty of space for plausible deniability, even if a good deal of what he wrote during the seventies seemed to gesture at intimacy. This is true of *Planet Waves* (1974) and especially that "break-up album" to end all, *Blood on the Tracks* (1975). Though Dylan's coyness has occasionally dipped as regards the latter, he can and has reasonably said that it had nothing to do with his by then tempestuous and crumbling marriage. *Blood on the Tracks* was, he claims in *Chronicles*, inspired by Chekhov stories and not his own life at all.[16] Years later, after, as Dylan put it, he came close to meeting Elvis (due to a rare infection around the heart), listeners thought they heard a man grappling with old age in *Time Out of Mind* (1997), but this too made him bristle: "People say the record deals with mortality—my mortality for some reason! Well, it doesn't deal with my mortality. It maybe just deals with mortality in general. It's one thing that we all have in common, isn't it?"[17]

Dylan's artistic decisions are statements against conflating his authorial and personal voices. Although we might take a psychological approach to the various periods in Dylan's oeuvre, it is also legitimate (and I would argue, favorable) to think about these variances—from folkie to rockstar to makeshift preacher to Frank Sinatra—as rhetorical moves. These epochs, including his finger-pointing days—to the disappointment of some politically engaged and wistful baby boomers—have been the result of studied decisions based sometimes on market desires and (mostly?) on aesthetic preferences. Though we can spin like dervishes trying to match the man and the period to see in these phases the mosaic of his soul, in fact what we have every step of the way are reflections of artistic discipline and control.

Dylan's iron grip is strengthened by efforts to separate subjectivities from artistic production. This dynamic is at least in part what appealed to him in the French poet Rimbaud, and in particular his tag "Je est un autre" (I is someone else). Dylan's connection to French symbolists is obviously formal and can help explain the phantasma-gorical quality of his work, the "visionary" qualities of his lyrics. The Rimbaudian *posture* is more important for us than any stylis-tic similarities. When Rimbaud uttered "I is someone else"—and who isn't at sixteen!?—it was part of a screed (a rhetorical exercise in itself) against his school teacher, Georges Izambard, and his inabil-ity to see beyond "subjective poetry." Rimbaud famously sought a "derangement of all the senses," a process by which he might become a "seer."[18] This talk resonates with Dylan's consistent suggestion of himself as a vehicle for material that exists outside of his control. As Ian Bell puts it, Dylan consistently peddles the notion that "songs somehow get written, albums somehow get made and fame—none of this is Dylan's doing—somehow descends."[19] In his interview for *60 Minutes* with Ben Bradley, Dylan talks about the origins of his songs from "that well-spring of creativity" and suggests (with a smirk and twinkle) that his early songs "were almost magically written."[20] His more recent stuff also comes from a mysterious place beyond the author's control. For *Modern Times* (2005), Dylan "just let the lyrics go," and as he sang them "they seemed to have an ancient presence."[21]

Of course, this kind of posturing does not amount to honesty or even coherence. And we shouldn't take the idea of objectivity or withdrawal as sacrosanct. There is little doubt that claims of detach-ment from his art are themselves indicators of a disposition and (pub-lic) features of a life lived. The so-called Never Ending Tour takes up many of Dylan's breathable moments, so performance for him is a way of life. Moreover, Dylan must want his shamanic qualities to be perceived as constitutional, or else he would not have (tacitly) endorsed Todd Haynes's film *I'm Not There*, nor would Jack Fate in *Masked and Anonymous* be a version of Bob Dylan (not Robert Zimmerman). Still, all this is of a different register than pouring out his heart and soul on stage and on records.

Dylan's distancing act is manifest on stage. Perhaps absence is the most remarkable aspect of his recent performances. At key points on any given night, he takes center stage with a harmonica not too far away. More often than not, however, he is a little hard to spot tucked behind a keyboard, sometimes a baby grand, on stage left tinkling away or pressing steady triplets. Any interaction with the audience (aside from the songs themselves) are miraculous, and when the curtain closes, he stands rocking back and forth in line with his band without pomp and circumstance and without anything like a solo bow—though he is always positioned in the middle.

This is of a piece with Dylan's infamous draconian prohibition of photography at his shows. It is hard to know exactly why Dylan is so adamantly against it: does he think it disrespects the music? Does he think photography steals a little bit of the soul? Is he a crotchety old man? Is he bummed that he isn't getting paid for the right? Maybe a little bit of everything; what's certain is that he cares. At a recent concert he spent some time scolding a Viennese audience: "Take pictures or don't take pictures. We can either play or we can pose. Okay?" He then stepped back and took a tumble. The effect of his disdain for picture takers and the extent to which venues enforce Dylan's desires ultimately rip his show from a modern context, the context of the cell phone, of promiscuous sharing. The policy is over-the-top, and that is the point; it is taken from the page of a distant past, an *imagined* realm of propriety and musical sacrality. Dylan seeks to cultivate an estrangement from his audience by means of a power trip that nevertheless has the effect of minimizing the player himself.

PERFORMANCE AND ITS POSSIBILITIES

While (Western) historical scholarship has long privileged written communication as its source base and preferred mode of communication, historical narratives come in many nonwritten forms. Today, with the softening of Eurocentric suppositions and in light of the return of orality (via, for example, audio and visual recordings) as a dominant communicative mode, the glyphic has lost some of its sheen. This pattern to embrace nonwritten communication, however, started in full force with the ever-richer analysis of "non-Western" cultures and the influence of anthropological methods, which focused on rituals to unearth the rules that govern various cultural units. The study of ceremony and ritual go hand in hand with the serious considerations of oral *and* performative means of signification.

Only recently, most pointedly within the (multi)disciplinary niche of "performance studies," has the embodiment of narrative and a whole range of gestural activities been understood as purveyors of history. This has been a notion taken up by Rebecca Schneider and Julia Taylor, among others. Schneider thinks about the captured gestural moment—a raised hand in statuary or a photograph—and asks whether this record of human movement is a "historical residue" and thus an "'object' that can be studied as evidence of continuity (continuity composed through repetition)."[22] An actor—or reenactor—may not be in any easy way a historian, but if in fact a performance does draw on physical and emotive traditions, the player on stage is not only a carrier of a gestural past but also a recombiner of gestures, and in this way they are part of a deeply a historical enterprise.

Dylan as performer is a topic that of late has become one of the most fruitful avenues for understanding the artist and his work, but the focus here is specifically on how it impinges on history making.[23] This section explores Dylan's vocal and corporal appropriations as well as the scenic and visual contexts that help him enliven the past.

Enrico Caruso, the Neapolitan tenor turned recording sensation and megacelebrity in the early twentieth century, continues to be considered a gold standard in operatic circles and, until Luciano Pavarotti came along to replace him, in popular consciousness. How strange, then, that a man who many have come to accept despite a voice David Bowie (lovingly) said sounded like sandpaper and glue, had the chutzpah to compare himself favorably to the tenor. In a moment of staged brashness at a press conference he pronounced himself "just as good a singer as Caruso." "You have to listen closely," he continued with ermine eyes, "but I hit all those notes, and I can hold my breath three times as long if I wanted to."[24] There's probably— and I mean this seriously—quite a bit to be written about Dylan's voice and operatic singing, but for now let's focus on Dylan's sense that his voice is capable of feats, that he can reach heights and depths, that if he wanted to he could play pulmonary parlor games past turning blue. His self-estimation—even if hyperbolically uttered—has no doubt encouraged decisions to change how he sings for years at a time.

In the vocal realm, as in many others, Dylan cares about imitation. In an homage to Stevie Wonder preserved at the Dylan Archive he lingers on the point: "He's a great mimic, can imitate anybody."[25] In general, the capacity to "do" other singers is a quality he's thought about carefully: "You can do anything with your voice if you put your mind to it. I mean, you can become a ventriloquist or you can become an imitator of other people's voices." He continues with some hesitation about his own powers, perhaps betraying a hint of humility: "I'm usually just stuck with my own voice. I can do a few other people's voices."[26] Everything Dylan pushes out of his own throat belongs to him, but not everything released sounds like his "authentic" or, better put, unique voice. That "thin wild mercury" sound of *Blonde on Blonde* (1966), the more lyrical approach with a just perceptible rasp of *Blood on the Tracks* (1974), the colorless drive and incipient pinch of his Christian period, are all evidence of phases in which Dylan consciously chose to shake things up but in a way that sounds (to the extent this possible) sui generis. His "originality" or "authenticity" at certain moments stands out because he has been so aggressively imitative during other stretches of his career.

Dylan's rise to fame was tied to his ability to take on other voices. His first record, *Bob Dylan* (1962), reveals a very young man already steeped in several traditions important to the folk scene: a man familiar with loads of songs heard late at night on the radio coming from Shreveport or Little Rock, stuff heard on recordings (some stolen, some borrowed), and, of course, things experienced at the epicenter of the late folk revival: the Village. The greatest influence came by way of his idol (once he moved on from Little Richard and Buddy Holly), Woody Guthrie, and further inspired by Ramblin' Jack Elliott (Guthrie's first obsessive imitator). But even early on, despite all the talk (then and now) about how he tried to embody Guthrie in mannerisms, affect, and vocal style, Dylan's first album reveals multiple interests. The Guthrie comes through in several tracks, including his talking blues number, "Talkin' New York Blues," in which his pretty clean phrasing allows the exploitation, as he says in the song, of a certain "hillbilly" sensibility, with its clipped words and squinched vowels. The link is most obvious in his "Song to Woody," where an Okie sensibility is paired with a tidy vocal line. Elsewhere, in "Pretty Peggy-O" he mixes an earthy colloquialism complete with audible half-chuckles and hints of a yodel with every "woo-hoo." However, when he sings "In My Time of Dyin'" Dylan transforms into the stereotype of a blues man somewhere in the Deep South, mostly through an affected gruffness, a rasp and a growl in the voice. "Highway 51" hits the listener with gravel and its affected Southern mannerisms: "fo' my time," "no mo'" (or "no moah"), "babay." He dips into and spits out final vowels; words drift away. Notably, the album ends with a rugged and ragged blues number, "See That My Grave Is Kept Clean" (picked up from a Josh White album) sounding like it comes from a man with the experience of ages—we hear the remnants of a hard life, stamped with, as David Yaffe says, forebodings of an "ancient croak" that he would grow into more naturally in later years.[27] When he was singing in his bare twenties, listeners imagined, as Dylan supporter and *New York Times* critic Robert Shelton did, that he was "consciously trying to recapture the rude beauty of a Southern field hand musing in melody on his porch."[28]

Another period of prominent vocal and phraseological borrowing started with *John Wesley Harding* (1967) and reached its peak with *Nashville Skyline* (1969), not even a decade after his debut album but already a couple of lifetimes away from it. The latter is a mishmash of easy-sounding country numbers mixed with the sensual "Lay Lady Lay" (originally intended for the soundtrack to *Midnight Cowboy*) and a more wistful, less intimate rethinking of "Girl from the North Country" sung with Johnny Cash. Especially after the steely affect of the midsixties, Dylan decided to turn toward a richer, rounder sound, a voice that Yaffe effectively describes as "part Hank Williams, part Pee-Wee Herman" or maybe Kermit the Frog. From whence this appropriated mellifluence, this good natured, knee-slap, aw-shucks vibe? Some people at the time suggested the voice reminded them of a contemporary, Charlie Rich.[29] More recently, musicologist Steven Rings has noticed a vocal homage to a fifties Elvis.[30] We don't need to identify the template but simply that this "new voice" hearkens back to something, and that something has little to do with the myth of Bob Dylan that had already congealed by the end of the sixties.

A long-lasting vocal shift came somewhere in the very late eighties/early nineties when, save for an artistically vibrant *Oh Mercy* (1989), things seemed to be going down, down, down. The period is remarkable for a pinched nasal sound, rhythmic squareness, phrases spit out with abandon, and little care for diction caused in part by a disregard for consonants. At its worst, a performance could be little more than undecipherable bleating. Perhaps Dylan's most notorious (and public) disaster came just before receiving a lifetime achievement award at the 1991 Grammys. Singing "Masters of War" at breakneck speed, not a word is clear and phrases start as if with a groan, as if constipated and looking for relief. For another, more successful, if still bizarre performance from that period, we can take a listen to Dylan's solo numbers during his thirtieth-anniversary concert at Madison Square Garden (1993), where, for example, "Girl of the North Country" is pitched accurately, though up the nose, and marked by speedy, unreflective, scarcely affective singing, a thing that must be taken whole as an artist's convulsion as opposed to the gentle thing it was and would become once more in later years. As many critics have noted, this period also witnessed what in retrospect seem to be two transitional folk albums—*Good as I Been to You* (1992) and *World Gone Wrong* (1993)—in which the prior vocal qualities remain, but many tracks are also marked by an intentional rasp, sometimes so guttural you can feel his phlegm shaking.

These are obviously aesthetic decisions that can be analyzed ahistorically, but there are historicizing elements nonetheless. Dylan's musical choices might leave the listener mystified unless one considers a kind of traditional approach to singing that Dylan may have been invoking, namely a slice of the blues, in which the word is secondary to sound and norms of beauty are flexible. In theory, he may have been hearkening back to a deep performative past, the sort described by LeRoi Jones (Amiri Baraka) in the context of African/ African American music marked by a hoarse and shrill sound.[31] Or maybe Dylan was bastardizing a kind of Appalachian whine.

It was not until the late phase of his career that the blues started fitting Dylan like a glove. Qualities honed during the previous decade remain: a certain rhythmic persistence, a driving and repetitive force that in its steadiness creates the possibility of playfulness, unexpected elongations and shortenings of the vocal line. Dylan relishes vowels, the possibility of curving the line, until he falls on hard consonants. Leaving behind keys that had long been too taxing, a more comfortable vocal positioning lets him grumble and growl without losing a little bit of a twang. In his voice, now, we are in the territory of the Delta Blues, this is Robert Johnson's realm, this is the land of Charley Patton, this is the home of Lead Belly, if any of these men had extra gravel in their tone. It is perhaps no surprise that only in the post-1997, post-*Time Out of Mind* phase Dylan starts to play "Blind Willie McTell" live and alive—far from the clean detachment of the 1983 outtakes (from *Infidels*), it now sounds what we imagine the blues sounds like, an archetype.

I say archetype advisedly. In evoking Blind Willie McTell, Dylan is not necessarily caricaturizing a certain blues vocal tradition, but it is striking to consider how little his current style has to do with the polished sound of McTell himself or of other greats such as Lead Belly, who was often quite lyrical in his musical approach (despite Alan Lomax's degrading desire to peddle a criminal fieldworker persona). Dylan is leaning on a "sonic color line" that plays on audience expectations, on their listening habits, to recall the blues genre, a genre that tends to be gendered (male, despite the importance of women to it) and racialized. But because he is not Black, the connotations of Dylan's performance are not subject to the same kinds of critical assessments as his vocal forefathers, who were carriers of "male sexuality, violence and desire," as so eloquently discussed by Jennifer Lynn Stoever.[32] In Dylan, as interpretive commonplaces would have it, the blues sound evokes the seer, the prophet, and the bard.

One of the most recent phases of Dylan's vocal career proves that his blues persona was just that. Dylan has been able to use more mellifluent styles when he has wanted to—take, for example, his "Working Man Blues #2" from *Modern Times*, a model of restraint and even sweetness. Most hints of iron and rust were left behind when he took up the American Songbook and sang beneath the towering shadow of a man he once called Mr. Frank (Sinatra). Listening to *Shadows in the Night* (2015) is an aural experience unlike most anything Dylan has done on record. Overall, we have as straitlaced an album as he has ever produced. It is, among other things, eminently honest to its sources: for example, the occasional use of lush horns (trumpet, trombone, French horn) implies an orchestral quality that gestures to old orchestral arrangements.[33] Dylan projects respect for the original compositions by rejecting the idea that he is "covering" them; to the contrary, he wants to "uncover" them in a way that is reverent, or at least not irreverent.[34] This requires creating a certain mood that looks back to the period that produced them. For instance, his closeness to the microphone evokes intimacy, a late night at a lonely bar. There is also beauty, depth, and resonance, a baritonal Sinatraesque quality, despite a fraying of the voice at the upper end of the vocal lines. Aside from moments of strain, especially in "Lucky Old Sun," the tone is elegant, his phrasing palpably restrained, a plausible homage from one Ol' Blue Eyes to another.

Dylan's voice is, of course, his own, with its virtues and deficiencies. But there is little doubt that at various stages in his career he was actively looking back at traditions that he could use and rearticulate. Dylan is by no means a simple ventriloquist or plain imitator, but he has those inclinations. He has certain tricks up his sleeve, certain vocal resources he can use, that are unique, but those can be manipulated to make historically evocative sounds. When Dylan goes out of his way to avoid self-referencing, the audience is left to piece together the whats, whys, and hows of the performance, something that functions as a distancing tool even as he invites immediate engagement. Vocal decisions imply self-effacement—the body is a carapace, the voice its own thing and not in any simple way Dylan's own—which requires the audience to think about what version of the past he is evoking even while being coaxed into that past through the wiles of a song sung.

Dylan is a songster, not a dancer, and yet he moves. Of all the musical, literary, and performative scholarship on him, relatively little has been written about movement as a way of conveying meaning. This is not the place to write that story, but clearly just as Dylan's vocal technique has not remained static, his mannerisms, his gestural rhetoric, is not stable either.

Folk performance was not known for movement, it was not about the body but about the voice, the nimble pick, and the piercing lyric. And yet, in the early days, source after source affirms, the performer—and his body—was never wholly out of sight.[35] Back then he dressed like a ragamuffin who had just tumbled out of a caboose—as Robert Shelton put it in 1961, his clothes were in need of tailoring: Dylan "has little to do with barbers and resembles a Holden Caulfield who got lost in the Dust Bowl."[36] Dylan's disheveled look was a studied experiment in humility meant to call attention to himself. In this he was emulating a performative schtick and he was aware of it as such because he knew that even Guthrie was pretending to be something he wasn't. But Guthrie was just one source. Dylan was twitchy on stage; before he started singing he would sit, fiddling with his guitar, tuning it, retuning it, offering several false starts, cracking self-effacing jokes. Witnesses say he reminded them of Charlie Chaplain. This quirkiness discarded the solemnity of folk music and maintained an earthiness that appealed to the Greenwich

Village crowd. When Dylan made it to New York City, Guthrie was in New Jersey slowly dying and Chaplin was well past his expiration date, living in de facto exile in Switzerland. Whichever way you look at it—and this went with the folk ethos—what audiences saw was a performer that in self-representation and gesture revealed layers of encrusted dust.

Perhaps Dylan's most mannered and intrusive use of the historical body came during his Rolling Thunder Revue tour (1975–76). With flowers in his cap, sometimes smeared in white paint, sometimes covered with a mask, the lanky figure on stage was meant to evoke something like a commedia dell'arte performer right out of some old European square, a world of mimes and clowns with their funny and melodramatic stories to tell.[37] To emphasize the point, Dylan sometimes appeared to be a marionette with his herky-jerky arm movements, as if he were loosely attached at the joints. It all had a strange quality, partly because it hearkened back to performative traditions that were not in any simple way American, and because the heyday of this sort of vaudevillian tic was long gone.

To an extent, Dylan's hippest period in the midsixties glanced back at the rock and roll flamboyance of his childhood idols, if much more stoned, but only many years later would that inclination take more recognizably historical forms. If you look at his performances after the midnineties through the early millennium, just as he was returning musically to the deep past, audiences sometimes saw a (much more wearied) version of Elvis with less pelvis, a type of bodily investment that evoked the world of the flesh that Ann Powers sees as a deeply rooted in American popular music.[38] The flick of the head up, one leg bent backward moving left and right, toes dug into the ground. When he still played guitar on stage, he crouched resting it on one knee, purposefully moving back and forth forty-five degrees, like a geriatric Chuck Berry. A little thrust forward now and then, and his guitar often just a little high above his hip, jutting out like the phallic thing that it is. Dylan is no jumper, there was no duck walk, but he was no longer the stiff vertical figure he could be during much of the eighties and early nineties.

Dylan's body was once again put to real theatrical (and historical) work during his brief Frank Sinatra period. Around 2016, what audiences got, apart from a show of American standards, was a man in love with a microphone. Center stage, he holds it, he presses against it, dips it like he's dancing. This is the world of the crooner. Take a look at his performance of "Once Upon a Time" at a televised Tony Bennett tribute (2016): amid some lapel tugging, he's intent on clinging to the mic stand at a diagonal, with his mouth almost melding to the mic itself. The whole thing must be a choreographed decision and one that really hearkens back to the archetype of a lounge singer, someone who might fit well in a Scorsese mob movie, a style that Bennett himself had long left behind.[39]

Again, there is a certain strangeness to all this. Strangeness, in that it forces the audience to engage with the performance from something of a distance. It is not what we expect of a modern performer, it is clearly an act, but an act with precedence. It is, on its most basic level, retro, and in that mode audiences witness the evocation of pastness.

☞

Performances need stages, and Dylan has stood on ones that have, by diktat of custom or authorial decision, historical resonances. In his early days he stuck to the conventions of the folk scene. Adornment was by and large rejected in favor simplicity, a singer hunched over a chair with guitar in hand, a spotlight, and not much else. Something akin to what the Coen brothers memorialize and fetishize in *Inside Llewyn Davis,* a dark, no-frills, misty room—the Gaslight in the Village—where voice and guitar are enshrined and intimacy with the audience is enhanced.

Simplicity was often coupled with rusticity. There are pictures of Dylan performing and hanging around Greenwood, Mississippi, in the summer of 1963 when the young singer was taken by Peete Seeger to get a taste of the South. In photographs and videos of a SNCC-sponsored voter registration event, we see Dylan in the fields, with overalled Black onlookers on the back of a pickup. Other images show him on the porch of a well-worn house with a triad of Black listeners and nonlisteners prominently displayed. A year later, in Newport, a town strewn with traces of obscene wealth, we have a video of Dylan sitting on a foldout chair, framed by the piercing eyes of Judy Collins, who herself looked like she would fit in a Dust Bowl photograph. Behind him a banjo-wielding old man and hanging foliage add a dose of the salty and the natural as Dylan intones "North Country Blues" with a plaintiveness that evoked a country both real and distant.

In the early days, on television appearances, Dylan was put in the past. Take, for example, his 1963 participation in a show hosted by John Henry Faulk, *Folk Songs and More Folk Songs* on WBC TV. Greil Marcus has beautifully described this show and its aspiration "to trace the whole sweep of American history." Faulk appears, pipe in hand, eyes cast dopily into the distance. Wistfully and with egregious folksiness, he spouts some homespun gibberish: "Whatever we have done as a people has always been turnin' up in song, folk songs we call em'." As he talks, with a map of the United states depicting an assortment of monuments from coast to coast—from California to the New York island—we hear a harmonica; soon we see Dylan singing "Blowin' in the Wind." He sings in front of painted blowing clouds behind him. In that same show, Dylan also sang "The Ballad of Hollis Brown." At first the camera shows some cartoonish mountains but soon moves downward to reveal an image of a cow skull (evoking a photo taken by the Marion Post Wolcott Farm Security Administration two decades earlier) before lingering on the almost-ominous shadow cast by Dylan's spindly legs.[40]

A year later, in a Canadian show, *Quest*, Dylan appears disheveled, singing in an old western bunkhouse. He starts with "The Times They Are a-Changin'," framed by a skylight and piles of logs. There are tough men everywhere, a man with a hook for hand takes a smoke, and from a different angle we see an older gent with a pipe between his lips using his hands to sew (a cap?). Dylan moves around the space for several other numbers amid some oil lamps, men going about their business, and photographs of old folks from a hazy past. As night sets in, some lounging men and empty cots signal the end.

Little more than a decade later, Dylan achieved a level of authorial power that he lacked at the start. How did he expend this possibility of freedom? The Rolling Thunder Revue tour, at least in its first incarnation, was purposely framed by overt historicism. This is evident in the concept of the show itself, an expansive and not terribly well-paid troupe of performers traveling around New England playing shows apparently (but not really) off the cuff, rejecting the "pop" veneer that so tortured purist rock critics of the times. Just on the eve of the two-hundredth anniversary of American independence, it was hard not to get the symbolic import of the tour's start at Plymouth, with photographs at the Mayflower replica there to tell the tale. Then there was the stage itself, starting with a curtain paying homage to the French film *Les enfants du paradis*, a film that takes place in nineteenth-century Paris amid theaters, performances, and lowlifes. The hurly-burly atmosphere of the tour, not to mention the cacophony of voices and, toward the end of each night, the crowding of bodies performing together, evoked the carnivalesque qualities of that film, or the carnival full stop.

The transformation of stage and backdrop would continue to mark Dylan's performances throughout the rest of the decade—cue, for example, his Neil Diamond/old Elvis run after the release of *Street Legal*—but a clear historicist approach would not fully reemerge until the new millennium. Starting at the very end of the nineties, and ever since, the emphasis has been on scenic sparseness and shadows. To be sure, Dylan's shows have plenty of the accoutrements expected of modern performances—sophisticated lighting and good(ish) sound—but there are no pyrotechnics. This inclination is most clearly on display in television appearances. His 2002 Grammys take on "Cry a While" finds him and the band squished tight in a stage within a stage, with muted yellow lighting casting the group's shadows against the background; the shadows are like ghosts, the performance as a haunting. This kind of aesthetic is fiercely protected against those who want a glossier sheen. When he performed at the Oscars (2000) via satellite, the producers wanted a sharp product; Dylan had to trick them into performing drenched in a grainy yellow. At times, his preferences can lead to awkwardness: when he played an old standard, "The Night We Called It a Day," for the penultimate episode of David Letterman's *Late Show*, things took a bizarre turn. The mellow light on Dylan, the nearly sepulchral darkness behind him, and the tight camera shot (seemingly a single camera set up as opposed to the multicamera norm) made for a poor backdrop. Dylan wandered to and fro, indeed, out of the shot itself, looking like he had checked out or needed to check in. However, his preferences can lead to things of unabashed beauty. Take, for example, his recent streaming concert movie, *Shadow Kingdom* (directed by Alma Har'el), which was filmed in a glossy black-and-white and set in a fictive club in Marseilles, France, the kind of place, as Sean Latham has put it, "made to feel like one of those places where the Blues began."[41]

HISTORY BY OTHER MEANS

I've been talking about the ephemeral, but there are other performances that will outlive Dylan, those that have been recorded and preserved for the ages.

Many who analyze Dylan's work have said he is primarily a live performer and only by chance a recording artist. It is a truism that, save for a few arguably overproduced records, his records have a "live," sometimes woefully underproduced quality (see the notorious production mess that is *Street Legal*). An important part of Dylan's own career narrative has emphasized how difficult it has been to achieve simplicity. He has not been shy about describing the lasting tensions he's had with various producers that come to a project with their own fancy ideas, none more than Daniel Lanois, the man responsible for the eeriness of *Oh Mercy* and *Time Out of Mind*. For Dylan, the purported quest for spontaneity is linked to ideals or the performance of "authenticity." With the passage of time, this notion has taken on historical qualities—Dylan's techniques are meant to hearken back to a tradition long before autotuning. He, for example, eschews overdubbing, uses a single microphone, and generally avoids any special effects. Jack Frost (Bob Dylan) has taken over producing duties for the last couple of decades and more, with the result of studied spareness and intimacy.

The record as object also becomes a vehicle for evoking the past. Most of Dylan's releases after *Time Out of Mind* (1997) contain artwork mostly reaching back more than half a century. *Modern Times* uses Ted Croner's 1947 photo *Taxi, New York at Night*, with its blurred, kinetic vision of urbanity. On the cover of *Together Through Life*, he takes us to the late fifties in a picture from Bruce Davidson's photo essay *Brooklyn Gang* depicting a couple making out in the backseat with a long road behind them. On the back cover, we have another black-and-white photo from the sixties of a "gypsy" band with players in action and the searing gaze of a dark man in a fedora wearing an upturned moustache. For *Tempest*, he goes way back with a late nineteenth/early twentieth-century sculpture of Athena found outside the Austrian Parliament building in Vienna. For his latest album, *Rough and Rowdy Ways*, the front cover has a color-tinted version of an Ian Berry photograph depicting dancers in front of a jukebox from a now-defunct club in East London (1964). Inside there's another tinted photo of Jimmie Rodgers and the Carter Family taken in Kentucky in 1931. The back cover shows a black and white shot of John F. Kennedy. Two albums from the last couple of decades show Dylan himself as a vision from the past. *"Love and Theft"* has him in grainy black-and-white in a recording studio, with tousled hair and a pencil mustache. The back cover has him looking a little like Guy Fawkes straight out of some strange yesterday as he grips an old-looking porkpie hat, wearing a smart suit and string tie. *Shadows in the Night* has Dylan depicted in a glossy black-and-white photograph split by bars on a blue backdrop meant to evoke an old Blue Note album. On the back cover, again in black-and-white, Dylan is sitting at a masque with a woman and holding a Sun Records single.[42] For his Christmas album (2009), in contrast with the wholesome sledding picture taken straight from the fifties on the cover, inside there is a painting by Olivia De Berardinis of Bettie Page in a gartered Santa outfit.

The discs themselves are artworks. The disc for *Time Out of Mind* has a label resembling the ones used by Columbia Records in the 1920s, complete with the advertisement of now antique recording technologies: "Vivatonal Recording" and an "Electrical Process."[43] *"Love and Theft"* evokes a forties and fifties Columbia logo, while *Together Through Life* goes back into the archives, advertising the "Columbia Gramophone Company." Of course, today it is very common for record companies to use original label designs for rereleases, but in Dylan's case we see the use of old art for new albums—we witness an evocation of old recording traditions whose time was well before the singer whose music we are listening to here and now. As Koji Matsudo has rightly suggested with reference to *Time Out of Mind*'s disc art: "Like a theatrical performance set in the past requires that props and setting remind one of the timeframe, the props used on this album may have been meant to remind the listener that it was set in the early 20th century."[44] But perhaps "remind" is too tame a word for what is going on; maybe Dylan's audience is confused into the early twentieth-century setting. They have to make sense of the artwork, they have to feel the dissonance to normalize it, and in the process they might experience the past.

Record and packaging decisions are of a piece with marketing campaigns. When Dylan released *World Gone Wrong* (1993), a solo acoustic album of old songs, Columbia records started to experiment with a publicity routine that would become common in subsequent years. The album's press kit underlined that the record was done "live . . . with no overdubs, much in the same way that Bob Dylan recorded in the early '60s." The pitch continues by highlighting that "the material draws on the old folk music and blues—some extremely obscure in origin—which have been at the heart of Bob Dylan's repertoire since his career began."[45] The record company is intent on hearkening back to Dylan's own back pages—this was, after all, before his "comeback" in 1997—while at the same time accentuating the album's rejection of modern technologies and its exploration of old and recondite things. Public relations or the art-ist's aesthetic? Probably both, but it doesn't really matter. Ultimately, all involved in this project created an aged atmosphere and provided the possibility for a historical experience.

Dylan, from 2006 to 2009 (along with a one-off reboot in 2020), undertook one of his most important recording endeavors as host of a radio show, *Theme Time Radio Hour.* Although the quirky program might seem peripheral to his work in general, such an expansive project (over one hundred episodes) should be considered, as John Hay says, "central, rather than ancillary, to his oeuvre."[46] The whole show, though on satellite radio, is populated by ghosts. In terms of content, DJ Dylan spins "records" from an array of musical tradi-tions that influenced him, and almost all the tracks are old. In pre-senting an American musical past, Dylan evokes programming by past curators of musical tradition, including, as mentioned before, Alan Lomax's several radio shows. As a radio personality, Dylan hones a speech pattern, an "old-timey voice with a Western accent," or maybe a geriatric Casey Kasem.[47] He comes prepared with dad jokes and a general comedic sensibility so at odds with what's avail-able in the world today: "I had a friend staying at my house recently. The other morning I came into the kitchen and saw him staring at a carton of orange juice. I asked him what he was doing and he said the carton said 'concentrate.'"[48] Maybe most importantly, from the start of each episode Dylan wants to re-create the atmospherics of pastness. A woman (Ellen Barkin) with sultry voice and voluptuous phrasing seems to appear with pendulum hips right out of a hard-boiled detective novel—maybe the femme fatale. The show suppos-edly takes place in Studio B of a nowhere city dominated, as a pro-motional poster shows, by the Abernathy Building (where the show is supposedly recorded) with its shades of gray and art deco touches. Through windows of the city's buildings you see stuff of everyday life, including a man at his (now mostly defunct) typewriter, and as if to make the point crystal clear, on the sidewalk a strange image of a skeleton (the past? Death?) puts on a fat man's suit (a costume?), bringing the dead to life.

There is a ludic quality to all this. But the intentionality and persistence of Dylan's efforts to create an imaginary realm that requires a glance backward and even invites the reader (mostly by aural means) into a new (old) *space* is part of Dylan's invocations of the past as an alternate truth to our current predicaments.

FROM THE PIECES

This chapter has dealt which how Dylan creates a sense of pastness. I've treated several techniques—cut and paste, performative acts, modes of estrangement—as discrete operations, but we have to imagine that these converge in complex ways to produce a historical effect. Many of Dylan's songs are stitched together to seem antique and are performed in similarly ancient guises (or are packaged in retro ways) to create a kind of distancing with the audience that requires them to calibrate modern expectations and old presentations. In doing this, Dylan is both interpreting old materials (lyrics, tunes, gestures) and repackaging them in a way that eschews newness.

This book does not intend to solve interpretive problems, but it's important to underline that Dylan's songs exist within this realm of historicized performance. Partly because Dylan offers no exegesis of his work, there is little guidance about how audiences should understand the historical elements they are witnessing. If his performances are historical reconstructions, are they objects to be looked at (listened to) as we would things at a museum, with a sense of their pastness, their separateness from today? Or are we to understand that the author has accepted, assimilated, and projected a version of the past?

Dylan is very aware of certain dangers associated with presenting the old for current audiences. In the latest installment of the *Theme Time Radio Hour,* he introduces Timmie Rogers's "Good Whiskey (And a Bad Woman)" (1946) with something like an apology. "Good Whiskey" is all about the malted beverage and the sexual pleasures that it induces with the right woman (loose, weak, bad, young). Dylan says,

Funny how times change. There are things in this next song that seem woefully out of touch today. For instance, Timmie Rogers, that's not Jimmy Rogers, that's Timmie Rogers, he wants an old whiskey and a young woman, and not the other way around, because he says, "Be sure you get a young chick, because gals do not improve with age." An adage he shared with Errol Flynn.

It would be easy to write Timmie Rogers off for such sexist thoughts, even in 1946, when this record was made. But consider this, he was also a groundbreaking comedian, considered the first African American to do an act that didn't depend on racist props, exaggerated caricature, or grotesque costuming. Most black comics dressed like tramps, and other types of low characters, so as not to be, as the club owners put it, too aggressive for the white audiences.

Dylan asks his audience to judge Rogers kindly because despite his retrograde ideas about sex, he was a revolutionary of sorts. The merits of his argument don't matter all that much for us, what matters are the complications inherent in an enterprise that raises the possibility of conflating performance and support for material being performed.

Dylan is likely sensitive to the problems posed by Timmie Rogers, in part because he himself has been criticized for his treatment of women in his songs. I don't want to step into this hornets' nest except to note that Dylan's form of historical recreation without a doubt evokes certain misogynist elements of the periods evoked, including forms of paternalism, masculine sexual aggression, and the espousal of a "whore/saint" dichotomy.

Take, for example, "Tin Angel" from *Tempest* (2012), a song rife with antiquated (or mostly antiquated) gender norms. The song deals with a love triangle, two men and a woman in between. These tangled relationships come to a head when the husband appears to confront his wife and her lover, leading to the death of all three. In the song, the woman plays the role of seductress, and both men blame her for their predicament. Her husband calls her a "greedy-lipped wench" while her lover dubs her "a murderous queen and a bloody wife." But for all her faults she ultimately manifests loyalty to her spouse, reminding her lover—whom she will shortly stab—that all "husbands are good men as all wives know." The song thus embraces tropes that place the female character in that fine line between femme fatale and good(ish) wife. The question for us as listeners is whether we should take the song as the faithful rendering of an old-style murder ballad or an embrace of musty gender norms.

Ultimately, the interpretive problem emerges from Dylan's will and ability to bend time, to perform history for modern audiences.

CONCLUSION

Dylan has never been too explicit on this point, but there is little doubt that his experiences of history making and his flexible conception of time allow him to imagine a time-travel effect. In this spirit he told an audience in San Francisco in the late seventies that he was going to give them an old song, "as old as I know. . . . So this is how I guess you call one of them old folk songs I used to sing. I used to sing a lot of these things. I hope it brings you back, I know it brings me back. This is 'Mary of the Wild Moor.' I guess it's about two-hundred years old."[49] It might be that Dylan wants to take the audience back to his folk days, but it is just as likely that he wants to take them back two centuries as well.

CHAPTER 3

"Sing in Me, Oh Muses"

Dylan as Mythmaker

We've now seen how Dylan works to re-create the past and even embody it. Here we continue the discussion of his history making by exploring one, perhaps *the*, important register of his historical work: the myth.

MYTHS

While in popular culture the concept of myth has gotten a bad rap linked to assumptions about falsehood and primitiveness, a defining feature of modernism depended on taking stories seriously. Origins and their manifestations in mythical forms were key to deciphering cultural essences. This sensibility led to the embrace of "primitive" art by people like Picasso, who saw, for example, African masks as objects of delight and as material to understand the very foundations of artistic expressivity. Closer to home, people like Jasper Johns—in works like *Flag*—trafficked on the embedded significance of primordial American symbolism, and Harry Smith's *Anthology of Folk Music* expected allegorical readings of spliced raw historical materials (old songs) deeply embedded in American culture. Joseph Mali has brilliantly argued that historiography conforms to aesthetic forms of modernism in its "recognition of myth as the primal 'order' in human life and history."[1] As a result, he argues, modern historiography is marked by special attention to myths of the past, which enable the understanding of past perceptions of reality. In the process of such historical reconstruction, histories themselves often project the myths that are being studied.

Folk songs often deal with real people and events, or people and events that *could* be real; in either case the end result is emblematic. Greil Marcus has talked about the smeared relationship between reality and meaning. He gives as a primary example the historical Stagger Lee, "Stag" Lee Shelton, who killed a man (Billy Lyons) in St. Louis in 1895. Marcus argues that "he had to be forgotten before his song could really travel. He had to become more real as myth than as a person, even when he was alive, even as he walked among the people who were already forgetting him."[2] This dynamic is inherent in the storytelling process when representation takes over the breathing being, even in a newspaper article, but it is doubly so when we're talking about the past, when all that's left are fragments to be imbued with significance.

Dylan would (probably) agree. In *Chronicles* he talks in some detail about what makes an individual or a narrative worthy of a folksong. He says, "It probably has something to do with a character being fair and honest and open," of embodying bravery "in an abstract way." He points out that Al Capone had success and notoriety but was not "interesting or heroic in any kind of way." Capone was frigid, a "sucker fish," he seemed like "a man who never got out alone in nature for a minute in his life." He was a bully, "not even worthy enough to have a name." Dylan contrasts Capone with Pretty Boy Floyd (the boxer), who "stirs up an adventurous spirit." Though he did not attain power, "he's the stuff of real flesh and blood, represents humanity in general and gives you an impression of power." That is, Dylan concludes with steely irony, "At least before they trapped him in the boonies."[3] Dylan leans on the idea of virtue that when married to verisimilitude, with something real and earthy, provides a message that emerges out of the particular and becomes universal.

The name of the game is "greater meaning." It is the quality that elevates (folk) music to a higher level. As Dylan has put it, "I find religiosity and philosophy in music. I don't find it anywhere else. Songs

like 'Let Me Rest on a Peaceful Mountain' or 'I Saw the Light'—
that's my religion. I don't adhere to rabbis, preachers, evangelists. . . .
I've learned more from the songs than I've learned from any of this
kind of entity. The songs are my lexicon. I believe the songs."[4]

We get a sense, a shadow really, of the exegetical, tropological
approach to his favorite songs in the bugged-out liner notes in *World
Gone Wrong* (1993), where Dylan tells us what the tracks are all about.
Of "Stack a Lee," that workhorse of a song mentioned by Marcus, he
goes on at some length and with studied logorrhea:

> It says no man gains immortality thru public acclaim. truth is shadowy.
> in the pre-postindustrial age, victims of violence were allowed (in fact
> it was their duty) to be judges over their offenders—parents were pun-
> ished for their children's crimes (we've come a long way since then) the
> song says that a man's hat is his crown. futurologists would insist it's a
> matter of taste. they say "let's sleep on it" but theyre [*sic*] already living
> in the sanitarium. No Rights Without Duty is the name of the game &
> fame is a trick. playing for time is only horsing around. Stack's in a cell,
> no wall phone. he is not some egotistical degraded existentialist diony-
> sian idiot, neither does he represent any alternative lifestyle scam (give
> me a thousand acres of tractable land & all the gang members that exist
> & you'll see the Authentic alternative lifestyle, the Agrarian one) Billy
> didn't have an insurance plan, didn't get airsick yet his ghost is more
> real & genuine than all the dead souls on the boob tube—a monumen-
> tal epic of blunder & misunderstanding. a romance tale without the
> cupidity.[5]

There's a lot here. Aside from the historical reading that he offers
to contextualize and explain the song, there is a didactic function as
well; this is a morality tale about the nature of truth, the quandaries
of fame, and real life versus the modern fictions.

Not surprisingly, Dylan's own work seems to radiate moral significance. (No one has done more to examine this than Christopher
Ricks in his magisterial *Dylan's Vision of Sin*[6].) This section contends
that to the extent that Dylan writes historical narratives, they very
often take a mythical form. At its simplest, myths can be defined as
stories with symbolic and allegorical meaning. Myths are everywhere
and are fundamental features within systems of communication in

which cultural materials convey meaning. Dylan's explicitly historical work doubles down on the symbolic and universal constituted by the concrete. Here I'll just point to a handful of representative examples.

LESSONS IN TALES

Maybe Dylan's primary form of (historical) mythologizing is articulated in biographies. The examples are many, including his takes on John Lennon, JFK, Emmett Till, Davey Moore, Hattie Carroll, Rubin Carter, etcetera. One of his most complex biographical reconstructions was written with Jacques Levy for *Desire* (1976), "Joey," about a Brooklyn gangster called Joey Gallo who was killed at Umberto's Clam House in New York's Little Italy. The song, although musically inert, is notable for its punctilious narrative, something it shares with that cinematic masterpiece on the same album, "Hurricane." The song reads roughly as a "rise and fall" story starting with Joey's entrée into the criminal underworld ("gamblin and runnin numbers"). There were gang wars, and a misunderstanding led to an attack on Larry, Joey's brother, whom Joey had to defend, leading to an all-out battle in which prisoners were taken. With hostages in hand, some wanted to blow up a building, but Joey steps in insisting that they are better than that. Such nobility went unrewarded, as the cops eventually got him on counts of conspiracy and he spent ten years in Attica, "reading Nietzsche and Wilhelm Reich," only to come out the other end a little lighter and looking like Jimmy Cagney. As an older man, he wouldn't carry a gun for the sake of the children, but despite his honor, Joey was blown away. The song ends with his family at the burial and with a scene of Brooklyn mourning.

For all the details, so concrete that it was surely intended to be understood as true, Dylan and Levy clearly had bigger fish to fry. The song is intent on both embracing the ambiguities, the grays of Joey's life, and on offering a response to extant myths about him. Though the song does not reject Joey's mob connections, it tries to weaken the fabric of gritty tales by suggesting these were just rumors or plain misrepresentations. When the family's criminal activities are mentioned, the lyric attenuates with "some say"; while people claimed that the fuse of gang war was lit by Larry's attack on another family, Dylan and Levy once again raise the possibility of gossip. When the police got Joey on conspiracy, it turns out it was all trumped up, they couldn't explain with whom he had conspired.

The countermyth Dylan and Levy provide is simple. In Joey we have the archetypal outsider who was misunderstood and abused. There wasn't any doubt that he was a gangster, but it turns out he was "caught between the mob and the men in blue." Whatever work he did for the family—and on this the song says nothing, really—his participation was not murderous but hardworking. After stopping the murder of hostages and bloody arson, Joey says, "It's peace and quiet that we need to go back to work again." Here the cops are villains, stand-ins for societal injustice and the shortcomings of the law. Elsewhere on the album Dylan takes up the plight of Rubin Carter, the boxer who was accused of murder, from the point of view of institutional racism, a theme picked up in "Joey" (with a nod to the complex racialization of Italian Americans) when he explains that he was friendly with Black men who understood being shackled.

There are other oppressors beyond the law, including other families, with whom Joey always dealt plainly and truthfully: he went without a pistol to the clubhouse of his "deadly foe." He was ultimately killed, but even in that last moment "he pushed the table over to protect his family." As Dylan would tell an audience more than fifteen years after *Desire* was released, "Joey" was "about a, sort of a, kind of a . . . hero of sorts. God knows there's so few heroes left."[7] Here we have the irresistible bad boy à la Tony Soprano.

Joey the martyr. Over and over again, the chorus lingers on paradox and senselessness: "King of the streets, child of clay. . . . What made them want to come and blow you away?" But even in death, the story goes on. At his funeral his best friend Frankie says he's just sleeping, a gesture at the sempiternal, his remnants despite physical death. And the story is not over even after the dirt was piled on—the song insists that those who killed him would meet their maker. Of course, the song itself is a testament to this as the past is rewritten to correct if not avenge, to celebrate and not condemn. It is a story as much about a man as it is about a system, or contrasting systems, of honor-bound criminals and corrupted justice of the legal and extra-legal kind.

Joey was a real man whose grave you can visit, but just as important in Dylan's oeuvre are those lives that are (possible) inventions that could be true. Of his early albums, there is an argument to be made that *The Times They Are a-Changin'* (1964) is his most "historical" both because it contains "With God on Our Side," a song that tries to rebuke historical falsehoods, and because four of the ten tracks focus on individual lives. Two of them, "The Lonesome Death of Hattie Carroll" and "Only a Pawn in their Game" (which deal with the assassination of Medgar Evers) are ripped from the papers, while the two others, "North Country Blues" and the "Ballad of Hollis Brown," are less verifiable.

When Dylan recorded "The Ballad of Hollis Brown," he was thinking in a historical mode. In a demo, he introduces it saying "This is, this, 'The Rise and Fall of Hollis Brown', it's a true story."[8] Dylan thus suggests that this story is in a sense greater than itself, placing it within a generic space of grand histories since ancient times and about ancient times that come under a "rise and fall" rubric. But in the same breath, he atomizes the story by underlining that it deals with a real person in real time and space. In fact, a listen to the song reveals that there is no rise in this rise-and-fall story, as Hollis Brown is down on his luck to begin with and only descends further into a craze—Dylan is being ironic (?). The value of his "rise and fall" statement is less about understanding the song and more about understanding a sensibility: Dylan's playfulness between the big and the small, the linked fates of empires and individuals.

The "truth" of this song is carefully constructed. Aside from the fundamental role played by the very act of naming—there is no Hollis Brown, but there might be—which evokes flesh and bone, other gestures toward biography are necessary for the narrative's propulsion: his wife and five children, his broken-down cabin. The rest of the story is littered with solid information about the troubles assailing Brown, the fruitless job search, the hungry children, the screeching wife, black grass, a dry well. All this builds the context for his decision to buy a gun and the "bleeding brain" that makes him use it to kill himself and everyone else. We are meant to bear witness to the tragedy. In the middle of the song, the narrator (and implicitly we too) switches to the third person as if talking to Hollis Brown himself. The song can only take place after Brown's suicide, so this is a phantasmagorical conversation or a time-traveling one.

The singer's detached coolness throughout is ultimately interrupted. The end of the song takes the story from a specific tragedy to its broader implications:

> There's seven people dead on a South Dakota Farm
> Somewhere in the distance there's seven new people born

The horrors of one existence disappear in an endless cycle of birth and death. This bloody scene is not unique, a fact borne out in other songs about the hard life of hard people in hard times, especially "North Country Blues." And so, even here where an explicitly moral or didactic tone is absent, we have that elusive Hollis Brown emblematic of a bigger story or of bigger significance than his own tragedy.

There are songs that are more about historical events than individuals. In the title track of *Tempest* (2012), Dylan burrows deep into the story of the *Titanic*'s demise. This fourteen-minute epic offers granular details, tableaux sketched with impressive brevity (even despite the song's overall uncommon length). References to both the real and the made-up evoke a textured past with an aura of truth. Dylan scatters historically verifiable nuggets, including temporal precision: "'Twas the fourteenth day of April . . .'tween the hour of twelve and one." He also mentions actual historical figures such as Mr. Astor (presumably John Jacob Astor IV). Other odds and ends that are pure authorial invention do not (generally) reach past the threshold of believability. There are descriptions of the ship and its materiality: shattered glass, alarm bells ringing, exploding engines, lowering lifeboats, flickering lightbulbs, swaying chandeliers, passengers flying about. Then there are interiorities that can only be the product of the imagination but that aim to convince: a bishop who tended to his dying flock, Jim Dandy who never learned to swim and gave his place on a lifeboat to a crippled child, Wellington's hard-beating heart, the captain reading from the Book of Revelations.

Dylan knew that these imaginative elements would be criticized, but he had a ready response. "A songwriter," he says, "doesn't care about what's truthful. What he cares about is what should've happened, what could've happened. That's its own kind of truth. It's like people who read Shakespeare plays, but they never see a Shakespeare play. I think they just use his name."[9] The specifics of an event matter less than those universal qualities that the artist can evoke through the art of creating possible pasts. Moreover, Dylan makes a distinction between the dead word on the page and the lived experience of the theater. One is artificial—or even fraudulent—the other is real. The "truth" is not beholden to anything fixed (or textual) but emerges from the *active* imagination.

Dylan folds myth into myth. The tune used for "Tempest" is borrowed from the Carter Family's "The Titanic," thus underlining the fact that the song is part of an extensive tradition of *Titanic*-related works (prominently sung in different guises by Lead Belly, Pete Seeger, etcetera). The other reference is, to an extent, subtler, and perhaps more intriguing. The song mentions (not once but twice) Leonardo DiCaprio, star of the blockbuster movie *Titanic*. Asked about this, Dylan responded with uncharacteristic (almost) clarity: "Yeah, Leo . . . I don't think the song would be the same without him. Or the movie."[10] Undoubtedly, Dylan is trying to establish a resonance between song and film. Maybe there is a musical link, too. Dylan's song sounds less American roots and more aggressively Celtic, arguably more like James Horner's famous *Titanic* soundtrack than the

Carter's plaintive approach. Crucial for our purpose is the very fact that both the traditional tune and the movie provide some of the filaments and the iconographical substance for "Tempest." In this way, Dylan's song is not only telling a story but also unearthing past *memories* about the event. In other words, just as the song itself is meant to mythologize the sinking of the *Titanic*, it articulates its past myths.

Unlike the movie, which is ultimately a testament to enduring love felt by the woman who survived because of her lover's sacrifice, Dylan's conclusion is (relatively) less maudlin. The lessons are likely many, but the song is clearly a contemplation of death. Dylan evokes a kind of danse macabre from medieval times, when Death (in the form of a spooky skeleton) was depicted dancing with commoners and kings alike: death as the ultimate equalizer. In light of such enormity, amid all the little lives consumed by the collision of ship and iceberg, only the biblical can offer an elusive kind of understanding, and so the captain reaches for the Book of Revelation. The *Titanic's* sinking is comprehensible only through that incomprehensible biblical text that is about end times and God's providential will beyond human reason. There is no feel-good ending, and how could there be? "Love had lost its fires /All things had run their course."

Dylan has taken on more expansive historical subjects as well. He did so mordantly early on in "With God on Our Side" (1964), a song that considers American self-imaging and projection as propounded by leaden textbooks. The song starts with the annihilation of Native Americans and passes through the Civil War and the two world wars, before arriving at the then present—on the cusp of real, possible combat with communist Russia. This story, as told in the history books, according to Dylan, was a providential one, with each American victory implying God's support. But, as the song reveals in its second half, all this is fool's gold, all *myth* in the worst sense of the word. In fact, it is a story told to galvanize, by means of hate and fear, militarism and militant bravado—this, to ensure that no questions are asked. The song finishes with a challenge to the listener, that they consider Judas's betrayal of Christ, implicitly its success, and whether or not there was virtue in it, whether he too had God on his side. He finishes on a pacifist note: "That if God's on our side / he'd stop the next war."

If this song challenges the pieties of an era, Dylan would write a counternarrative two decades later in "Blind Willie McTell" (1983), a marvelous song written during a blighted decade in Dylan's career, though it did not make the cut for *Infidels* (1983) to the befuddlement of just about everyone. It is ostensibly about a blues singer whom the refrain suggests was totally unique, and yet the song isn't about McTell himself but about the blues, a point scarcely worth stating since it's been said before. The idea is written into the fabric of the song with its appropriation of "St. James Infirmary" and the evocation of the musical genre in every stanza. But more than a musical genre, the blues is constituted by and in turn constitutes the American experience. It is a textured world of bootleggers, gypsies, chain gangs, and East Texan martyrs, too.

Perhaps the most powerful moment of the song comes in its (original) central stanza. In it, Dylan describes burning plantations and cracking whips and the "ghosts of slavery's ships," a searing image that, as Christina Sharpe has elegantly discussed, can stand as emblematic for the Black experience, even though she reminds us that we are dealing not with ghosts but with a living past.[11] From one form of traumatic violence to another, Dylan also describes the moaning tribes, the untold death that made America what it is, sung in funereal tones and accents, far from any rosy providence. This is the underbelly of America's past turned up in full view.

God does not escape the song's grasp. We get that sense from the very start when Dylan uses an image of arrows on a doorpost, which, as Michael Gray points out, evokes *Exodus* and the marking of Jewish homes in lamb's blood to spare them from God's punishments: "And they shall take of the blood, and strike it on the two side posts and on the upper door post of the houses, wherein they shall eat it."[12] Most importantly, at the end, after his tour of America's (cultural past), Dylan underlines a (supposed) truth about human desire for what is rightfully God's—grace?—despite man's profound sinfulness, his lust for "power and greed." There is nothing honorable about the version of America he has told; it is a story of sin.

Given Dylan's known interest in the Civil War, he was bound to write a song about it. "'Cross the Green Mountain" (2004), written for a (mediocre) Civil War film, *Gods and Generals*, focuses squarely on one historical event, though admittedly one of enormous consequence. Dylan, as ever, blends realistic and fantastical perspectives. The song begins in the realm of the imagination: the singer asleep by a stream, victim of a monstrous dream that "swept through the land of the rich and the free." The visionary is blended with a real land, a real country. Beneath the surface of the reverie, Dylan provides concrete marks of authenticity—mention of the "Atlantic line" and later a battlefield in Alabama—that evoke place. The song then frequently gestures at real sights and sounds that savor of authenticity: burning altars, foes crossing battle lines, miles of ravaged land, the letter sent to a mother telling of her son's bullet wounds, all elements already deeply ingrained in the American imaginary through pictures, songs, movies, etcetera. The song is also loaded with ambient scenes meant to be transportive: chilled skies and frozen grounds, ringing bells, and blazing flames.

But above and beyond the tools used to establish verisimilitude, the song is fundamentally about a way of thinking; it reconstructs a series of sentiments that propelled men to battle. The singer reflects on the world's grayness and on how life's lessons would blossom from man's toil (in war). Combat would ensure that pride and glory would be buried beneath enduring virtue. The warrior fights in hopes that people will one day say he "was loyal to truth and light." As ever, Dylan is quick to conjoin secular virtues with divine ones. The singer exhorts, "Serve God and be cheerful, look upward . . . beyond the darkness of man." Such language leads Ian Bell to marvel at how, "in a few bare lines," Dylan can summon a "nineteenth-century notion of sacrifice on the 'altar' of war, of the 'good' Christian death for one's country."[13] So what's being reconstructed here is a whole mentality, a cultural and intellectual orientation that allowed for promiscuous violence; Dylan is repackaging and re-presenting a logic appropriate for its time, or, put another way, he is evoking the unifying mythologies that left so many dead.

The song also promotes sentimentality. This is not a history of facts but a history of feeling that he has favored since his younger years, when he lamented that history was cold and lifeless.[14] The singer lingers on brotherhood, the bond cemented by common gumption and belief in a cause. He describes looking into the eyes of a "merciful friend," and in the face of inevitable death he is moved to think about "the souls in heaven who will meet." Dylan unveils the love and mutual admiration beneath the stony faces of young soldiers.

In a brow-raising footnote, the most recent editors of Dylan's lyrics (through 2014) suggest the possible connection between the song's first line—"I cross the green mountain"—and epic poems from Kosovo that speak of Milan of Toplica, a fictional Serbian nobleman who fights and is wounded in civil wars after crossing green mountains.[15] The strange suggestion was, according to Christopher Ricks, in the spirit of a quip, but it is nevertheless significant given the fact that Dylan's song is written in a heroic register recounting aspects of civil strife that speak to the "essences" of battle, those aspects that can be appropriated by either side and both at once.[16] The song is an expression of a national myth that is undoubtedly multivalent, but no less powerful for that. Just as medieval Serbian epics provided the cultural memory that could lead to crimes against humanity as recently as the 1990s, so too the epic of the Civil War serves as an important space of memory in which current battles are fought. The point here is that Dylan uses forms of historical evocation to say significant things on a higher plane.

Interestingly, "'Cross the Green Mountain" portrays a Civil War without slavery. The conflict seen through the lens of the battlefield leaves race out of the picture, a point that deserves some consideration.

Dylan believes the Civil War is fundamental to the American experience and to his own work. In *Chronicles* he says that during the 1860s "America was put on the cross, died and was resurrected." This understanding was a fundamental source of inspiration, and he goes on to say that the war and its "godawful truth" would subsequently "be the all-encompassing template behind everything I would write."[17] Dylan is no apologist for one side or the other, and he does not see the point of picking favorites. In a telling passage, he reveals that Ray Gooch (Dylan's creation) lamented that New York City had won the Civil War and that "the wrong side had lost, that slavery was evil and that the thing would have died out anyway, Lincoln or no Lincoln." Dylan thought that Gooch's words were mysterious and bad, "but if he said it, he said it and that's all there is to it."[18]

Dylan claims to be less interested in who was right or wrong and more about how people of the times configured their reality. When he visited the New York Public Library and studied nineteenth-century newspaper sources, he was primarily interested in the rhetoric employed by contemporaries. He realized, among other things, that the "issue of slavery was not the only concern." People then worried about "reform movements, antigambling leagues, rising crime, child labor, temperance, slave-wage factories, loyalty oaths and revivals."[19] Aside from criticizing the naiveté of painting the Civil War as the product of the slavery debate alone, Dylan also recognizes the common coordinates of the American mentality, North and South. Reading the papers, he claims (in an homage to Lincoln's second inaugural address) that "everyone uses the same God, quotes the same Bible and Law and Literature."[20] So—maybe—North and South are the different sides of the same coin. In an interview with Mikal Gilmore he mentions an article from the *Pittsburgh Gazette* "where they were warning workers that if the Southern states have their way, they are going to overthrow our factories and use slave labor in place of our workers and put an end to our way of life."[21] Gilmore prods Dylan as if to make sure that he doesn't let the South off the hook: "But there were also claims and rumors from the South about the North." Dylan agrees and mentions tropes about states' rights and implicitly their errant belief that the North was out to abolish slavery in any simple way: "The North just wanted them to stop slavery, not even put an end to it—just stop exporting it. They weren't trying to take the slaves away. They just wanted to keep slavery from spreading. That's the only right that was being contested. Slavery didn't provide a working wage for people. If that economic system was allowed to spread, then people in the North were going to take up arms. There was a lot of fear about slavery spreading."[22]

Ultimately, whichever way you looked at it, and despite all nuances, Dylan is very aware that the country "burned and destroyed itself for the sake of slavery." And even beyond the Civil War, he has a strong sense that slavery is the original sin of the nation. This is a stigma, he says, that America will never get over. Dylan exudes a sense of loss, because had slavery not been at the core of the Civil War, "America would be far ahead today." He marvels at the iniquity of racism and calls it a "distraction," presumably from some purer future or purer past. Race is not, but should be, beside the point—something he has argued since his youth. As a young man receiving the Tom Paine Award from the Emergency Civil Liberties Committee, he expressed impatience with racial discourse: "And they talk about negroes, and they talk about black and white. And they talk about colors of red and blue and yellow. Man, I just don't see any colors at all when I look out."[23]

"'Cross the Green Mountain" is not a textured analysis of the Civil War or its causes. In it North and South are on the same plane, indistinguishable. Perhaps in the exclusion of slavery, race, and politics, there is a tinge of melancholy for America's best instincts denied, and in this it expresses longing for a history that never was, an (inherent?) unity frittered away. Perhaps the virtues on display are meant to stir the aspirations of the listener, and those aspirations are meant to be colorblind.

"'Cross the Green Mountain" is not alone in excising, or at least undermining, racial elements. Indeed, a song we've already looked at, "Blind Willie McTell," is perhaps the most salient example of this dynamic. In the version most often sung today, and the version on his website, Dylan rejects the stanza mentioned above dealing with slavery and the murder of Native Americans, in effect, the most historical part of the song.[24] The sense that the blues and the States were born in the shadows remains, but any racialized aspect of that birth is diminished. Could it be that the stanza in question was *too* concrete for a song Dylan intended to be more elusive and atmospheric? Could it be that the blues itself, intended to be a stand in for the nation, was undermined as a symbolic force amid the concretion of the past?

Much earlier in his career, Dylan's "Lonesome Death of Hattie Carroll" experienced deracialization. The song treats the death of a maid, Carroll, as a result of William Zantzinger's mistreatment. Carroll was Black, though the song does not mention it once. Mike Marqusee dismisses this detail, telling us that no one in 1963 needed to be told the race of either person. This might be true, but Dylan *does* tell us that, for example, Emmett Till was Black ("The color of his skin was black") and does talk about overt racism in songs like "Oxford Town" ("All because his face was brown . . ."). Something else is going on here, and I suspect it has to do with the mythological register I have been talking about in this chapter. In many of Dylan's "topical songs" (that might be taken as historical enterprises as well), Dylan is speaking to a concrete present, but with "The Lonesome Death of Hattie Carroll," he is seeking something more universal through the lens of a particular story. It is the story about a society unwilling to mete out justice equitably—in this case, Zantzinger basically goes free (only six months in jail) because he came from the patriciate of Maryland. The song is also an attack on all the cogs listening who allow society to function in all its unfairness. It is an attack on those who, as the song says at the end of each descriptive stanza, "philosophize disgrace, and criticize all fears." Dylan orders them to "take the rag away from your face, now ain't your time for your tears." The targets of this finger pointing are, as Marqusee puts it, "the supercilious liberals who offer their sympathy . . . but little else."[25] Even more broadly, of course, this is a commentary about the chasm between thought and action. Perhaps a young Dylan believed that amid this moral reckoning, race was, again, a distraction. The situation as archetype, as *myth*, is what matters most . . . at least this time.

CONCLUSION

Dylan's songs have all been interpreted for their symbolic, even iconographical, qualities. This chapter has wanted to underline that his "historical" songs function on two levels, one concrete, the other less so. These songs are about specific events, all with a sense of truth conveyed both by the depiction of real occurrences and by providing forms of descriptive detail that beckon verisimilitude. However, these songs are more than the plotting out of a true story; they have a moralistic quality to them that universalizes the specific. This is history not only as a narrative form but also a didactic one, where there must be a lesson, a moral to be learned. Moreover, it is worth thinking about how these lessons can, in certain circumstances—the trope of the good gangster, the virtue of war, the Americanness of the blues—be reflections in themselves of historical mythologies being repurposed and reinserted into a popular historical idiom.

CHAPTER 4

"There's Something Happening Here . . . Mr. Jones"
Interpreting Dylan Historically

If Dylan thinks about, has been influenced by, and practices history, his work is also read in that register. In a sense, this whole book is a testament to the fact that at least one audience member (me!) recognizes this, but as anyone who has read anything about Dylan in the past couple of decades knows, I'm not the only one. I don't think the issue of historicity has been explored sufficiently (thus this book), but viewers, listeners, and readers have, to varying degrees, experienced and intuited Dylan's historical enterprise. Traces of this are evident in some of the (anonymous) fan testimonials sociologist William Barry collected on his website, mybobdylanstory.weebly.com. One person notes, "He's [Dylan] quite obviously well read and alludes to visions of our mythic forgotten past and archetypes." Another suggests that "Bob's work seems to touch base with musical history even as he (re)creates it in real time in a new way. Bob's music is a synthesis of old and new." The result of this oldness and newness provides, according to another fan, "special insight into the history and American music." There are more grandiose claims as well: "He is tapped into the psyche of Americana and relays that to his fans."

This chapter is not a comprehensive study of how Dylan's work is perceived, and it pays little attention to what the broad base of his fans think. Instead, it offers a handful of perspectives from a restricted and, to an extent, aleatory group of scholars and critics who suggest interpretive possibilities available to viewers and listeners. I'll explore historical readings of Dylan's work to reveal some ways that his historical activities can connect performer and audience. In that connection we get a deeper picture of the historical culture that binds them.

IS IT TRUE?

Dylan sneers at sticklers. He sometimes believes, as seen above, that artistic truths and stuff in history books proper are different and not equal. Art has the upper hand. This, for now, doesn't matter: the sticklers do. Living as we do in a world where truth and fake truth seem indistinguishable, arbiters of what is really real are still around, even (and maybe especially) when it comes to art: cue all those articles trying to save us, the nodding masses, from accepting a movie or a streaming series as real. More often than not, at least within the realm of entertainment media, such discussions explicitly or implicitly deal with contested versions of the past. By means of dissemination and subsequent discussion, these re-presentations of history are triggers for popular historiographical discussion. Much the same can be said of Dylan's work, which implicitly, perhaps unwittingly, invites listeners to assess and engage with discussion of accuracy. Describing this dynamic reveals not so much Dylan's historicizing affect but his audiences' willingness to play the history game.

Take, for example, "Joey" from *Desire* (discussed for other purposes in chapter 3). In a *Rolling Stone* review of the album from 1973, David Marsh proclaims, "The record only falters, in fact, when it attempts to write or rewrite real history." He is incensed by Dylan's rehabilitation of a vicious mobster, not simply because it is faulty in details but also because the singer does not soften the image of the right kind of criminal. Marsh recognizes that the song fits the pattern of romanticized outlaw discourses, in which the hero robs from the rich and gives to the poor. Proper history has shown that the glorification of people like Billy the Kid and Pretty Boy Floyd are inaccurate, but their myths are morally justified and so "their canonization at least makes a kind of sense." Dylan's elevation of Gallo, according to Marsh, is based on thin moral ground: "Joey was heroic because he spent his time in prison 'readin' Nietzsche and Wilhelm Reich, because he came out of prison dressed like Jimmy Cagney." There is nothing heroic about this antihero, nothing worth conserving, intellect (Nietzsche and Reich) and charisma (Cagney) notwithstanding. This is a grossly simplistic reading of the song, but the critique is interesting in how accuracy and its licit vagaries are dependent on the subjects' virtue. Dylan's supposed moral naiveté in this case renders his efforts to "forgive" Gallo unforgivable. The song's "neatest ellipses," Marsh claims, "is to avoid all mention of the public execution of Joseph Colombo, which the evidence suggests the Gallo mob ordered." He continues, "Gallo was an outlaw, in fact, only in the sense that he refused to live by the rules of the mob—it's as hard to be sympathetic to him as it is to be comfortable with Robert De Niro's crazy Johnny in *Mean Streets*."[1]

Desire also contains arguably Dylan's most famous and most beloved real-life song, "Hurricane." The track takes up the accusation of murder against Rubin "Hurricane" Carter, a washed-up boxer, then imprisoned for a crime he claimed he did not do. This song, above all others in the Dylan canon, is marked by emphatic activism, both on behalf of a wronged individual and, more broadly, against a decrepit American legal system. The song's much-vaunted cinematic qualities lend it a special vitality, a realistic resonance that is, of course, redoubled by the fact that Dylan was on a mission to vindicate Carter and that he stitched together the song from news reports. The song's claim to truthful truth and its acceptance as such by many inspire and, to an extent, require listeners to engage with matters of accuracy. The contestation of Dylan's interpretation of events landed him in court. Patty Valentine, who found the bodies of those allegedly murdered by Rubin, is mentioned in the song, and that same Valentine sued him for defamation, claiming that Dylan had (unfairly) impugned her. Dylan's defense rested on the aesthetic qualities of Valentine's name and the thread she helped strengthen in the song's narrative. Years later, those who believe in Carter's guilt still rail against the song, which they think has presented a false narrative, a contention that was reawakened when the song was included in the soundtrack and in promotion for a feature film, *Hurricane*, which was also subject to intense scrutiny based on its imaginary flights. Michael Gray might be right in claiming that "almost every line of Dylan's song is inaccurate," but this matters less than the obvious role "Hurricane" has played in opening up a space for considerations of historical truth—a space broadening even today as Carter's case receives fresh attention (in the form of a podcast).[2] One reporter talking about the rebirth (or recrudescence) of the Carter case rightly says that the "wrongful-conviction story was immortalized in Dylan's song."[3]

From the impersonal to the personal. Even songs that have nothing to do with the public record have been mined to better understand Dylan himself, or vice versa, the biographical is meant to inform the meaning of any given song. This is the stuff of fandom, but not only so-called Dylanologists play the game. Speculations of the biographical seep into any discussion of any given song, questions that cling like barnacles to a stone. Even the most(ly) even-handed, arguably the most elegant biography of Dylan by Howard Sounes—*Down the Highway*—digresses into these hypotheticals, wondering, for example, who the girl is in the "Girl from the North Country"—surely, he posits, one of Dylan's youthful loves from Minnesota ("where the winds hit heavy on the borderline").[4] The inclination is, importantly, not reserved to Dylan's more realist songs, but is a strong current in analysis of his whole oeuvre. Thus, we wonder whether "Sad Eyed Lady of the Lowlands," a song expressionistic and symbolist in flavor, is about Dylan's then girlfriend (and future wife) Sara Lownds.[5] Such considerations help us understand, on the level of reader perception, the ways in which mostly imaginative material is turned into a verifiable past, regardless of authorial intention.

THREADS AND TRACES

There are subtler ways in which Dylan's work inspires people to think about history. Sean Wilentz's *Bob Dylan in America*, among many other things, reveals how Dylan's songs elicit from audiences a special kind of historical filter, how he invites listeners into rabbit hole and how fans gladly oblige. At core, Wilentz's book poses a series of questions to place Dylan's work into broader contexts, to understand how Dylan uses scraps of Americana, and how this process tells us something big about America itself. He asks: "What do those tangled influences tell us about America? What do they tell us about Bob Dylan? What does *America* tell us about Bob Dylan—and what does Dylan's work tell us about America?"[6] The book offers myriad answers to the above, many based on close readings of songs written or performed by Dylan in tandem with discussions of the musical tradition from whence they emerge. More than musical genealogy, Wilentz sometimes excavates the true stories behind certain songs, mostly *not* in the spirit of checking Dylan's accuracy but of recreating and invoking the slice of America that served as background and impetus. So, for example, a chapter that deals broadly with Bob Dylan's "Blind Willie McTell" describes the song's genesis, provides an analysis of the song's historical elements, and reveals the resonance between Dylan and McTell's approaches to music making. The chapter also spends a great deal of time on McTell himself, his relationship to traditional music forms, his recorded legacy, and elements of his biography. The chapter switches from one singer (Dylan) to the other (McTell), establishing parallels that at various points are pulled together into tight knots.

Elsewhere, in a chapter that considers Dylan's performance of a blues number, "Delia," from *World Gone Wrong* (1993), Wilentz deals with the ways in which the recording says something about Dylan's trajectory, his relationship to traditional music, and more specifically how his version compares to older versions of the song. To do this— especially the latter—Wilentz spends time discussing the "real" Delia, what the public records say about how she was murdered by her lover, and the racial politics that the story reveals. Though only a sidenote to the chapter, Wilentz also touches on the truth, highlighting how Dylan's version, as with all preceding ones, leaves out key elements of the story, "the saddest facts of the original case: the tender ages of both Delia and Cooney, the utter waste of their young lives." But what the song loses in factuality is overcome and recompensed by the feelings evoked, how Dylan "adds pathos to an old blues song."[7]

Daniel Wolff's recent book, *Grown-Up Anger*, can also be taken as exemplary of how Dylan's work paves a path for the historical imagination, this time in part because of his connection to Woody Guthrie. The link between Woody and Bob is an old warhorse and has been nurtured by Dylan himself. Looking back on Dylan's imitative "act," Wolff breaks new ground by tying historical threads: he follows both men's stories and connects them to labor history, especially the history of mining in Michigan's Upper Peninsula, mostly through the lens of the 1913 Calumet massacre. The links between these three elements—two folk singers, labor, massacre—are rendered real, but not in any obvious way. Wolff dresses his book in a cloak of the *unknown* and says it is about "a string of interconnected mysteries."[8]

The full richness of *Grown-up Anger* can't occupy us now, but its premise or inspiration is crucial. One of the lynchpins between these three stories are two songs with the same tune, Guthrie's "1913 Massacre" and Dylan's "Song to Woody," which represent the connection between the two singers, the story of the mentor (by means of recordings) and mentee. These songs imply a musical genealogy, but they also reveal a folk process and a sensibility, which insisted that folk music should sound old, "the older the better." These aural artifacts were supposed to emerge from a purer time inflected by populism and repulsed by mass market appeal. This sentiment united Guthrie and Dylan (for a time) and reveals a musical moment in which truths were spit out into the world and in turn required examination on that level.

Guthrie's song described a version of a 1913 tragedy that took place on Christmas Eve, when over seventy miners and their families, many of whom had previously been on strike, were crushed to death as they tried to escape the hall when somebody yelled "fire!" All the details of the event—including who yelled—remain unknown and unknowable, but in Guthrie's telling, following a contemporary account, the culprit was a minion of mining fat cats. To get to this story, Wolff works backward from Dylan's evocative music and his historical gestures, not to mention Dylan's own midwestern upbringing, to the life of his predecessor and then to a tragic past that preceded them both. Here, again, we have musical traditions, folkways, taking a critic/historian back to a version of the truth.

This dynamic is depicted emblematically by the book's cover. Here we see the young Dylan looking and posing like Guthrie, who appears in a (smaller) picture beneath him. Both of these pictures rest atop an image of workers lining the burial plots of those killed in Calumet. Dylan and Guthrie can thus be seen as standing over or emerging from a "real" past that, by means of the folk tradition, can travel through generations. Reading and portraying these interconnections is surely, at least in part, a result of a kind of folk engagement that depends on establishing resonances and ligatures between past and present both on the level of artists and of history writ large. The book cover reminds us of this, in the same way that photography from the new millennium (2010) inspired Matthew Frye Jacobson to reflect on the loop of past and present within the context of folk protest: "A folk guitarist at the head of a throng of Occupy marchers conjures Phil Ochs's 1960s just as surely as he does Woody Guthrie's 1930s." We can easily replace Ochs with Dylan and this would still be mostly true.[9]

Especially, but not exclusively, within the context of Wolff's book, it is clear that the road into the past depends not only on Dylan and Guthrie in themselves but in an aurally perceivable filiation. Just as Guthrie's "1913 Massacre" was laced in the dust of an old English ballad, so Dylan's quotation of Guthrie tune almost demands a historical approach. This, despite the fact that Dylan's "Song for Woody" is in no way a protest song or a historical narrative but a gentle tribute to a musical forefather. Those embedded in folk circles (then and now) expect to sniff out musical borrowings; an assumed intermusicality sends the auditor in search of what went before.

Importantly, such explorations go beyond unearthing the materials, the bits and pieces, Dylan has appropriated. Some listeners use those appropriations as paths to lands unknown, to the pocked and rocky territory of the past. We should take this kind of engagement and apprehension of Dylan's work seriously because, while (historical) truthfulness and creativity do not always overlap, Dylan's work compromises that dichotomy and in turn deeply affects whoever cares.

TRANSFIGURATION, REVISITED

As we saw in chapter 1, Dylan talks about his own transfiguration and implies that such an experience is not unique to him. Who has been transfigured and what does it all mean? Dylan insists he has no idea: "Who knows who's been transfigured and who has not? Who knows? Maybe Aristotle? Maybe he was transfigured? I can't say. Maybe Julius Caesar was transfigured. I have no idea. Maybe Shakespeare. Maybe Dante. Maybe Napoleon. Maybe Churchill. You just never know, because it doesn't figure into the history books. That's all I'm saying."[10]

It's hard not to laugh at the purposeful opacity. And it takes some effort not to fall into the trap of trying to figure it out. Here, though, what matters is not what Dylan believes but how the historical possibilities he spouts are then appropriated by us, his obstinate observers. If we take seriously Dylan's belief that man can be transformed and that the stage might be the site of this possibility, then he as the body on stage can become something else, and that thing is evocative of the past.

Richard Thomas, a classist by trade, is one of very few scholars to take Dylan's talk of transfiguration seriously. Where Dylan implies that he experienced something along the lines of some (ill-defined) spiritual transformation, Thomas brings the discussion back to more comfortable and traditional scholarly ground. "In my view," he says using classic academic code for uncertainty, "the process of 'transfiguration' that Dylan explores . . . is more or less the process literary critics call 'intertextuality', perhaps an intertextuality of characters in the song as much as the straight texts themselves."[11] By evoking the concept of intertextuality, Thomas suggests that Dylan's various borrowings and personae are techniques meant to elicit active comparison between texts (including performative texts) and their sources. This is precisely the way many literary scholars approach their interpretive work, and this is an important facet of audience reception.

Things get a little less straitlaced when Thomas discusses the thematic interrelations between Dylan and the Roman poet Ovid. Thomas specifically discusses the ways that Ovid "transfigures" himself into Odysseus, the archetypal wanderer, in his poems of exile (the *Tristia*). At first, Ovid's comparison is humorous, as he points out that his lot is harder than that of Odysseus—Odysseus at least got help from the gods. Moreover, Ovid is quick to point out that unlike the "fictitious" stories of Odysseus, his own pains "are anything but myth." Thomas is skeptical about the accuracy of this distinction between a fake past and a true present: Ovid's claim "could be truth or untruth, with either being well and good." With this ambiguity in mind, Thomas himself adds a layer of uncertainty by claiming that Ovid ultimately takes the comparison further "and has more or less become Odysseus" by recounting his own journey.[12] Thomas might be speaking metaphorically or accentuating the effects of the intertextuality, but what do these purposeful comparisons (Thomas's and Ovid's) tell us about the effects of the purported rhetorical games—what affective reality is the poem (and Thomas's take on it) trying to elicit?

Things become more complicated still when Thomas claims that Dylan, by going back to Ovid who hearkened back to Odysseus, was himself actively courting transfiguration. Thomas traces Dylan's connection to Ovidian texts to evoke a kind of morphological resonance. Dylan follows Ovid's lead by presenting himself as Odysseus and does so in a particular way. Thomas emphasizes how, throughout *Tempest* (2012), Dylan's references to Odysseus are culled from a speech given by the mature hero, "whose identity the characters in

Dylan's songs, and Dylan himself, are taking upon themselves." To further flesh out this analysis, Thomas points out that when Dylan sings those *Tempest* tunes live, he does so with a statue of the river goddess, Minerva, the same likeness (if not sculpture) on the cover of the album from whence these songs come. Why? Thomas suggests that it is because "Dylan transfigured into Odysseus, the wandering survivor of so many blows, quite naturally has with him a statue associated with the goddess, has taken her on as his divine patron."[13]

Thomas continues this thread into Dylan's 2017 Nobel Lecture. There Dylan lingered on *The Odyssey*, one of three books he says "have stuck with me ever since I read them way back in grammar school." After a brief description of the troubles and strife faced by the hero, Thomas says he makes the parallels between the ancient wanderer and himself. Dylan says, "You too have had drugs dropped into your wine. You too have shared a bed with the wrong woman. You too have been spellbound by magical voices, sweet voices with strange melodies. You too have come so far and have been so far blown back. And you've had close calls as well. You have angered people you should not have. And you too have rambled this country all around. And you've also felt that ill wind, the one that blows you no good. And that's still not all of it." The "you" in this passage, according to Thomas, is Dylan himself and in this way he is "confirming his transfiguration, and listing a few of their shared experiences."[14]

Thomas's take on transfiguration is at once playful and (consequently) ambiguous. Thomas is eliding the notion of transfiguration and intertextuality, terms and ideas that in fact are not equivalents. He creates for the reader a real terminological problem, which can be resolved only if we assume that the author is not being wholly forthcoming. At least on the level of Thomas's rhetorical choices, there is something else going on, something more than borrowing tunes and snatches of words. Thomas claims that "Dylan imagines and creates the world that he inhabits in his songs and in performance."[15] Here we hear faint echoes of a possibility implied in previous chapters: the incantatory powers of performance and Dylan's ability to channel antiquity by means of artful borrowing. At least on a level of possible meanings, Thomas kicks open the door, revealing Dylan as alchemist, archive, and conveyer of history itself.

These transformational and evocatory possibilities are so often mentioned that they are on the verge of becoming tropes. Jonathan Lethem, as noted at the very start of this book, expresses with writerly elegance something many of Dylan's followers (not in the cultic sense) intuit, that "Dylan seems to feel he dwells in a body haunted like a house by his bardlike musical precursors."[16] Lethem suggests that Dylan ultimately dissolves into the realm of symbol and signification as a conduit for musical traditions, his body as a vessel for spirits. Although keeping it mostly academic and certainly more concrete, Wilentz's take on Bob Dylan *in* America is about transformation with certain quasimagical qualities as well. As touched on before, he argues that Dylan is a teller of American tales that can be taken literally or symbolically but that are ultimately "constructed in America, out of all its bafflements and *mysticism*, hopes and hurts" (my emphasis).[17] The effect of this is ultimately that in performance (live or otherwise), Dylan melds the old and the new to the extent (and this is where a hint of the magical comes in) that "the present and the past feel like each other."[18]

Taking a cue from Dylan, critic Greil Marcus latches on to the suggestion that after immersing himself in the folk tradition, he started to feel like he was actually part of the songs he was singing. Marcus claims that Dylan is capable of performing "a transference" of his own embodiment to the listener.[19] This notion of transference is fundamental for understanding why some people believe that Dylan can summon an American past.

Such transportive possibilities emerge from Dylan's tactical choices, but these have to be engaged with the susceptibility of the viewer and listener. There is no greater observer of Dylan and his work than Marcus, so it is worth lingering on how he perceives Dylan's historical work. In a 1991 article for the *San Francisco Chronicle*, "Dylan as Historian," Marcus takes on the theme directly. He focuses on "Blind Willie McTell," a song that "makes it clear that his [Dylan's] greatest talent is for bringing home the past, giving it flesh." The effect, he suggests, quoting the ethnologist H. L. Goodall, Jr., is that the song allows or insists that the listener experience not only their own lives but also "the lives we don't lead."[20] The song is to an extent exhortatory, the singer's witnessing of the various tableaux depicted "demand that the listener witness, too: see, hear, and *smell*."[21] Beyond what the song says, its rhetoric invites searching for a deeper meaning by deciphering the resonances it shares with traditions long gone. Though he doesn't use the word, Marcus's analysis of the song lingers on intertextuality, the layered echoes in words and notes, that Dylan provides. He underlines how Dylan's piano keeps "a tricky, unsettled time, sometimes flashing up and rattling as if the Mississippi bluesman Skip James is back from the dead to play the keys." Pushing beyond the obvious musical debt Dylan's song pays to "St. James Infirmary," Marcus ties the song to a recording of Richard "Rabbit" Brown's "James Alley Blues." Marcus exploits weak tendrils of commonality, a frailty he does not deny. He admits that the identified ligatures are not due to a shared melody or even to Brown's style but that the connection lies in the "spirit" shared by "James Alley Blues" and "Blind Willie McTell": "Brown's preternatural, bottomless strangeness, seemingly the voice of another world, right here, where you live, the prosaic dissolved by faraway ominousness, a sense of the uncanny, an insistence of paradox and curse."[22] This analytical stretch is important, both because, again, we are in the realm of the incantatory and transformative, but also because it is a reminder that the "reader" matters a whole lot. Marcus does not deny that his takes on various cultural artifacts are subjective.[23] His claim about the link between Brown and Dylan is as much a response to what Dylan is doing as to what Marcus wants to believe—the author, as Roland Barthes would have it, is dead.

For someone like Marcus—and not only Marcus—Dylan's revivalism punctures any semblance of time's linearity. Take Marcus's recent analysis of the "Ballad of Hollis Brown," the song discussed above about a man who kills his family in hopeless times. He doesn't use the word "transfiguration," but he talks about its kin. Throughout the song, Marcus says, Dylan performs something strange—"you feel not what the singer is feeling, but what the character is feeling, but he is no longer a character." This is an effect of Dylan's ability to write and perform from the inside, from Dylan's feeling that he has in fact become a character from his own songs (and from songs that are not his own). This first transformation or embodiment is then conveyed to the audience.[24] There is no singer, there is only a character, a sense of instantaneity, a sense that things are unfolding before your eyes: "What is about to happen hasn't happened yet, because there is no past, there is no future, there is only the unfolding moment, where Hollis Brown stands frozen by choice, and anything is possible."[25] Beyond the story and its frozen time there is the musical artifact, and this too is marked by multiplicity that is both grounded in time and not: "'The Ballad of Hollis Brown' is three songs: Bob Dylan's song; the folk song; and his song that sounds like a folk song, authorless, written by history and weather, no original and no copy."[26] This is hyperbole at its best, but it nevertheless gets at the important notion that Dylan's work is perceived as a product of historical reconstruction; the author is present, but he is also a conduit for the raw sources, and as such what the viewer ultimately gets is an "authentic" narrative or representation of the past.

So, Dylan as performer and songwriter is perceived to be a great invoker, a walking history book. But this is not only a matter of form; form provides an avenue for historiographical analysis.

DEEPER MEANINGS

Marcus is part of that first wave of critics to emerge in the aftermath in the sixties when rock and roll turned into "Rock," a respectable thing for people to write about. Dylan played a major role in facilitating that respectability, and the airs put on by that venerable species of critic. A number of people have written more about Dylan, but Marcus is among the few to place him within the broad sweep of music history and (American) history tout court. Indeed, few critics display such an acute historical imagination, and few have written such overtly historical work. As hinted above, Marcus's sense of history is elastic and thoroughly subjective. He is driven by a willingness to time travel (rhetorically at least), a penchant elegantly described when, for example, he discusses efforts to imagine himself walking through the same streets in Berkeley where Harry Smith spent his days. His efforts to jump into the past clearly provide a context for his understanding of Dylan's transportive qualities and help explain his general inoccupation with cause and effect or any stuffy historical enterprise. Too cool for that. Indeed, he is happy to accept frankly specious claims that music can both represent and actually shift the tectonic plates of the past. In this way, he is—as many historians are—both a student and a propagator of myths, even if he has suggested that there is a contradistinction between myth and history: "History without myth is surely a wasteland: but myths are compelling only when they are at odds with history. When they replace history they too are a dead end, and merely smug."[27] This is a smug statement in itself, a nice turn of phrase that pretends to establish borderlands that Marcus very seldom respects. In fact, for him myth often *does* replace history, or makes a mockery of it, at least. He plants himself on the page with the authority and gravitas of an eighteenth-century man of letters, conjuror of nations, believer in the "spirit" of a people.

Witness one of his more nonsensical claims, made plausible by rhetorical niceties. Marcus describes Stanley Booth's assessment that Carl Perkins's "Blue Suede Shoes" "represents one of the most important steps in the evolution of American consciousness since the Emancipation Proclamation" and that "at a distance of thirty-five years, a generation, it can be seen as the prelude to a tragedy, the murder of Martin Luther King, one of the '60s assassinations from which the country has not recovered." Marcus fully agrees and poohpoohs skeptics along the way: "It is this sort of sweeping affirmation that always brings forth a chorus of skeptics happy to forsake the mysteries of art and culture for the facts of entertainment: *How can you make so much of a song?*" Marcus answers the straw man, "because it isn't simply a matter of the right notes at the right time . . . rather it's a matter of hearing the notes with a vastly enlarged sense of place and time. It is the echo of those notes carry of a promise and a threat as vast as one can find in 'Blue Suede Shoes.'"[28] I cite this at some length because it reveals the fudging of myth and history that is central to Marcus's work—a song is taken not only as emblematic or symbolic but verifiable and truthful; it is on the same plane (almost on the verge of causational entanglement) with the future music can presage. I don't agree with much of what Marcus says—even if he says it all exquisitely—but the point here is not about agreement, it is about interpretive lens. In pasting together the realm of myth and history Marcus meets Dylan on his own turf.

So, what does Marcus make of Dylan's historical efforts? To an extent, we've already answered this in suggesting that he buys Dylan's time travel and even time effacement fully, wholly, and with zeal. But what version of America does Dylan evoke?

Because Dylan functions as synecdoche for the folk tradition in general, we can start to answer this question by Marcus's (and Wilentz's) take on the American ballad, the prototypical folk narrative mode enshrined by Francis Child so long ago. What do the ballads say about America? "That it's a place of great stories and storytellers, for one thing. For another, that the sardonic bard, the sly salesman, the trusting soul, the hopeless fool, the heedless lover are all of a piece: all in some way talk the same slow, deliberate language; all call out to each other, and to the country at large . . . it says that our nation—dedicated to the proposition that liberty is real—is obsessed with death: the death of actors in the ballads; the death of the nation itself as a field of liberty."[29] From these songs we hear the voice of an America split within itself, a place of dereliction and hope, of oppression and freedom, of newness and obsolescence.

This kind of analysis assumes that old ballads are dependable primary sources. These are, in other words, the materials that feed the gaping maw of historical analysis. Dylan's work obviously serves different purposes. Dylan, through performance, has done the historical heavy lifting, he has processed original materials. When Marcus and others see versions of America found in Dylan, the analytical process veers toward historiography or the study of what historians have said.

Marcus's take on Dylan Town: a liminal world, the world of the self-made man struggling with a puritanical order established by the pilgrims, by prophets of the city on the hill.[30] Unsurprisingly, for a man of Marcus's time, the American spirit is defined by the outsider, it is the breath of self-made people on the edges of everywhere who flip off imposed pieties. This is a thick thread in Marcus's iconic interpretation of the "Basement Tapes": its tracks contain old and old-sounding music, a fictional Smithville, a land "haphazardly constructed out of the past, out of Smith's *Anthology* and the like, out of the responses people like Bob Dylan, Mike Seeger, and so many more brought to that music, its stories, and to the world—another country—implicit within it." As he puts it, "The vanished world they incarnated—as history, a set of facts and an indistinct romance, as a set of artifacts, as a work of art, completed and finished—was going to die and you were going to be the last witness." These representations and incantations were both acknowledgments of the past and its finality, but paradoxically also resuscitations, or better put, reincarnations. The performer, says Marcus, certifies "that a certain race of people had vanished from earth, which is also a way of testifying that they once had been at large upon it—and as a result of your witnessing, what traces these people might have left behind were to be lodged in you."[31]

So, what is this Smithville that Dylan and the like evoke and ultimately inhabit (or by which they are inhabited)? What is this race of man, of minnesinger whose echoes remain? It is a land of fatalism, of remorselessness; the frontier town "with the guilt and doubt of utopians and perfectionists no less present in the air than the free rapaciousness of traders, con artists, and killers." "Everything," Marcus waxes, "seems open, any turn can be made at any time"—until it's not.[32] Elsewhere, in his discussion of "Highlands" from *Time Out of Mind* (1997), Marcus turns things on their head; despite the geographical gesture of the song, this is not Smithville, but an "unmapped country . . . hanging in the air as a territory of danger and flight, abandonment and discovery, truth and lie, but as 'Highland' plays, there is the sense that no one has been there for years. The singer has long since traversed that country, but he can do without it."[33]

Either way you look at it, by means of archeology and historical re-presentation of significant old materials, Marcus's interpretation takes us to a land on the edge of immensity—this is the frontier, where you either meet your end or seize the future. In tone and substance, Marcus silently evokes Frederick Jackson Turner, who at the end of the nineteenth century influentially argued that the uniqueness of American culture, that American democracy itself, emerged from the frontier where, of necessity, rugged men forged their independence and rejected the fripperies of the Old World. In the Geat Out There, according to Turner, there was a world of individualism and free competition, the will to start afresh without the preconceptions and conditions frontiersmen left behind. The frontier enchanted others, including nineteenth- and early twentieth-century folklorists, principally John Lomax, whose work on cowboy songs meant to evoke the tough guy, "bold young spirits" who "loved roving; they loved freedom; they were pioneers by instinct; an impulse set their faces from the East, put the tang for roaming in their veins, and sent them ever, ever westward."[34] Visions of these brash men with frontier dreams were of a piece with another turn-of-the-century perspective that was more hesitant, nervous, weary, and wary. The frontier mentality had been transformed—the frontier was ultimately taken, the country had become a nation, the individual had, to an extent, been subsumed within that construct. Changing contexts required the convergence of old ideals and present needs. As in Marcus's work, in those transitional days some underlined the dangers of renewal, a specter of the end of something great; but there is hope as well, the power of man to find *new* frontiers.

Dylan is thought to live in this world of ambivalence. In prose less elevated than Marcus's, historian Douglas Brinkley gets to the point: Dylan is an "old-style American individualist." It is a land of giants such as Walt Whitman and Chuck Berry, "of border towns and murder ballads," where Dylan may now be "the last man living there."[35]

TRICKSTER

In her review of Martin Scorsese's documentary *Rolling Thunder Revue: A Bob Dylan Story*, Ann Powers begins by repeating a near-truism: "Bob Dylan is messing with you." As Powers suggests, the film about Dylan's most storied tour is framed by Dylan's claim (as articulated in the film) that "you only tell the truth when you are wearing a mask." This is of a piece with Dylan's insistence on reminding audiences, as Powers puts it, that "American voices always engage with myth-making, hucksterism and strategic lies." Thus far: Dylan. But as Powers goes on to reveal—and as has been hashed and rehashed at this point—Scorsese's movie is in on the game. Fact and fiction are blurred, as are "magical myth and droning reality." Important people from the time of the tour are excised from the story, footage from the tour and contemporary footage used for Dylan's flopped movie *Renaldo and Clara* are intermingled, and there are talking heads that were either not at the events being discussed or made up altogether.[36]

The film can be swallowed whole. You see Sharon Stone claiming falsely to have followed Dylan on the road during Rolling Thunder. You see a made-up Jack Tanner, a supposedly young congressman who scores some tickets for the tour with a little help from Jimmy Carter. Most entertainingly you see Stefan van Dorp, a pretentious European filmmaker, who supposedly took footage of the tour. These creations—and much more—on closer scrutiny reveal their fraudulence, but they "work" because those characters and situations maintain a semblance of truth.[37] Isn't it believable that a rock star would have quickly developed some sort of a relationship with a young, beautiful fan? Isn't it possible that Jimmy Carter—a Dylan fan—might have had access to Dylan's management or the man himself? Wouldn't Dylan, the wannabe auteur (director of *Renaldo and Clara*, after all), seek the cinematic assistance of some avant-garde European?

This is what matters to us here. Scorsese is not only reading and regurgitating Dylan's hucksterism, but in that reading he is seeing Dylan's approach to the past, he is imitating a mode of historicizing.

After all, isn't Scorsese's film a history in its own right? So, through it we can see Scorsese's comfort with Dylan's posture as teller of (past) tales, a world of could haves and should haves so rich and sticky that it overpowers the straight truth as we might conceive it. If Dylan's work sends people down memory lane, it's worth keeping in mind that viewers and listeners can also be in on the game.

CONCLUSION

Whether or not Marcus or anyone else in this chapter is right or wrong in their assessment of Dylan doesn't matter. This chapter points to a style of reading Dylan's work that is profoundly historical and that is in tune with the mythical elements of Dylan's songwriting. This type of engagement is not wholly or primarily attached to the myth of Dylan himself; it is not the consequence of his singing old songs—most of the time he is not—nor is it a consequence of the biological fact that Dylan is now an octogenarian songster. If the historical lens with which some critics approach Dylan's work is not inherent to the performer, what we've seen here is an engagement with activities—musical and performative—understood and parsed by their own rules of representation that allow for varied understandings of any song's meaning by individual interpreters. Of course, this dynamic is not exclusive to Dylan and his audiences, but it is notable in this case for its historicity, its historiographical qualities, at least some of the time. The fact that Dylan is thought to be recombining and appropriating cultural materials to re-present the past in the form of narrative on the page or performance suggests that his output portrays some sort of truth, be it of the artsy-fartsy kind or of the more pedestrian fact-based vintage. He is thus an intermediary, a great evoker, a spirit with powers of time travel who inspires others to flex their historical imagination.

CHAPTER 5

"Blood of the Land in My Voice"

Dylan's Authorial Persona

Arriving here, we are at the precipice of a conclusion. Having now followed a loose tale that started with the historical culture that produced Dylan to the historical culture that reads him historically, this chapter (briefly) considers the position from which Dylan "writes" history. This chapter follow's historian E. H. Carr's advice that we should know the historian—the bees in their bonnets—before we read their work. Since this book has stayed far from the biographical, I will (mostly) not change course here. Dylan's life is less important to us than how he fashions himself as a performer and how he articulates his place within the (musical) tradition to which he belongs. This is essential for understanding Dylan's authorial stance, for figuring out the perspective he assumes, and consequently something about the past he seeks to portray.

I CONTAIN MULTITUDES

In his latest album, *Rough and Rowdy Ways* (2020), Dylan focuses on combinations and permutations. The first track lifts a little Walt Whitman when he sings, almost in the land of affected afterthought, "I Contain Multitudes." Though (lyrically, not musically) nuanced and dense, there is a simplicity to the song as well; it borders on a trite statement on the varied origins of artistic inspiration. The singer puts himself among the poets, Edgar Allan Poe and William Blake, and among the musicians, the Rolling Stones, Beethoven and Chopin, too. But artistic debts are not the only ones being paid here. Dylan is grasping at, or better put, pointing to a mythical realm, or myths themselves that help construct the singer. This is most obvious when he mentions Anne Frank and, in a strange juxtaposition, Indiana Jones. Asked about such name dropping, Dylan performs Dylan:

> Her story means a lot. It's profound. And hard to articulate or paraphrase, especially in modern culture. Everybody's got such a short attention span. But you're taking Anne's name out of context, she's part of a trilogy. You could just as well ask, "What made you decide to include Indiana Jones or the Rolling Stones?" The names themselves are not solitary. It's the combination of them that adds up to something more than their singular parts. To go too much into detail is irrelevant. The song is like a painting, you can't see it all at once if you're standing too close. The individual pieces are just part of a whole.
>
> "I Contain Multitudes" is more like trance writing. Well, it's not more like trance writing, it is trance writing. It's the way I actually feel about things. It is my identity and I'm not going to question it, I am in no position to. Every line has a particular purpose. Somewhere in the universe those three names must have paid a price for what they represent and they're locked together. And I can hardly explain that. Why or where or how, but those are the facts.[1]

Striking statement, if ambiguous. Dylan doubles down on the idea that the song is threaded like tapestry and that individual lives can be woven to create a greater image, a lasting impression. The sum of all its parts emerges from a song-making process that reflects the author. Against what he has said on many occasions, here we have admittance of an autobiographical element to a song and as such it takes us deeper than usual into an explicit realm of self-fashioning, a recognition that the self is made up of many borrowed parts.

"My Own Version of You" picks up a similar theme, but this time creation is externalized. The song's conceit is based on Mary Shelley's Dr. Frankenstein and his powers to give life. The singer starts by matter-of-factly telling us that from summer to winter he's been visiting morgues and monasteries in search of body parts to make a human. Whether the object of the song is metaphorical or real or both is hard to tell; what's clear is that this new being results from a promiscuous blending of cultural elements—Al Pacino's Scarface and Marlon Brando's Godfather; Leon Russell and Liberace and John the Apostle; Jerome and Saint Peter; Freud and Marx. The result is a creature from time out of mind, a creature that reveals the human race in its face. The newly formed monster is not only a revealing symbol but it is needed as a medium, the proverbial lens through which to see what is out there. The singer asks his creation to show him the light at the end of the tunnel and to search for it standing by a cypress tree that had been there since Roman times, before the Crusades, and before America was ever created. In the singer's creative act, in this futurity, there's a path back as the song falls to its end: "I want to bring someone to life—turn back the years / Do it with laughter—do it with tears."

Dylan emphasizes the extent to which the recombination of old materials allows us to keep one foot back there from whence they came and one foot in front of what they create. (Self-)creation is a project of expansiveness and border crossings, a result of sensitivity to time and timelessness: past, present, and future converge in the creation of a monster—the old parts, the new creation, and what's next. Chronologies remain distinct until they are not.

Attunement to his multiple origins and those of his songs has been crucial to how Dylan frames himself as a musician. Over the years, he has insisted that there is no real way to pin him down, there is no single (musical) tradition that informs his own output: "I always liked rhythm and blues and country-western—for as long as I could remember I never really separated one kind of music from another. I even liked polka."[2] Dylan's output has reflected this fact as he has moved with relative ease from folk to rock to country to Tin Pan Alley and even polka in "Must Be Santa" on his Christmas album, *Christmas in the Heart* (2009) (not to mention a polka-tinged cameo for the sitcom *Dharma and Greg*).

Musical generosity is at the center of Dylan's *Theme Time Radio Hour*. Because each episode is driven by a single topic—baseball, cars, whiskey, etcetera—there needn't be, nor could there be, an emphasis on one artist or one style. As some have suggested, the varied acts on the show represent something about Dylan's own inspirations, but the show is also making an implicit argument for the elasticity and eclecticism of American music itself. Here is a musical world without clear timelines (although most of the stuff presented is old), without much attention to generic boundaries, and a similar inattention race, which, for more than a century now, has been an integral component of generic definitions.[3] Especially on the latter point, Dylan's avoidance of strict borders feels like an implicit argument or reflects what Germans call "the art of omission." In other words, Dylan goes beyond suggesting that he has many influences to projecting the implausibility of American musical history chopped up into discreet pieces.

This inclination to tear asunder musical barriers of genre emerges from, or at least fits comfortably within, current musicological trends. In a move that closely resembles postcolonial analysis and its emphasis on the role hegemonic powers (say, the British Empire of the nineteenth and early twentieth century) have had in arbitrarily segmenting subjects, musical styles are products of cultural and capitalist considerations. Out of a complex blend of genres and interlaced artistic interests, record companies and executives carved up music to serve (and create) different markets—thus country, folk, and blues, among other forms that were part of an integrated musical lexicon increasingly became (arbitrarily) distinct.

Importantly, these divisions have racial origins. The blues, for example, was defined as Black, and country as white. The most racialized form of direct marketing led to the production of "race records." There is a strong argument to be made—and Guthrie Ramsey, for example, has made it—that there is something we can call a specifically African American musical tradition and to deny or obscure this possibility, to insist on the artificiality of racial divisions in music, runs the risk of implying that there was some (relatively) color-blind (musical) past, or at least a color-blind possibility.[4] However problematic this might be, Dylan has adhered to the better side of this interpretive framework from his earliest days: as we've seen, to him racism, and even the concept of race, is debilitating. As discussed above, Dylan is acutely aware that slavery and racism are fundamental aspects of America, but he sees these as a deviation from the natural order, thus their sinful quality.

Dylan's efforts to get back to a purer world (that never really existed) is creatively rendered in one of his most powerful and oft-performed late-career songs: "High Water (For Charley Patton)" from *"Love and Theft"* (2001). If he has sung songs by many "blues men," he has rarely been as explicit in his quotations than when he evokes Charley Patton, a first light of the delta blues. The choice is no doubt linked to a musical genealogy important to Dylan, but there are other aspects that make Patton a useful symbol. If he can be a placeholder for the modern blues, he is an equally important emblem of the genre's complexities. There is a musical story here, namely, as Elijah Wald points out, that Patton in fact was equally at home in what might be considered preblues forms as much as in what we now consider the blues proper. But part of Patton's richness as synecdoche for the blues also rests on his many-sided identity. For one, he is a useful figure to Dylan because he evokes anonymity. As Dylan well knows, Patton recorded under the name "Masked Marvel," a name Dylan would have seen printed early on in Smith's *Anthology* evoking a time when who a singer was was beside the point. But, of course, Dylan does refer to the man himself by name, and this too is significant. Though it is not wrong to call Patton a Black performer, in fact, his own ancestry was and has been the subject of much speculation. There has always been talk of his "mixed" racial roots that includes white, Black, and Native American blood.[5] Davis "Honeyboy" Edwards claimed "he was a yellow mulatto, with curly hair," and Howlin' Wolf Burnett said that "Charley Patton was more Indian than Negro. He was a half-breed, you know."[6]

Specific racial classification is less important than the fact that Dylan is grappling with issues of race when evoking Patton and by, in effect, becoming him. "High Water" is (among other things) an evocation of Patton both in its title (an homage to Patton's "High Water Rising Everywhere") and in performative mimicry. For example, Dylan is particularly generous with his hard-edged growl, a quality preserved in Patton's recording. Aside from musical style, Dylan plays with the possibility of embodiment. Greil Marcus rightly points out that a 2008 photograph of Dylan with a floppy tie and general weighty demeanor seems based on the only known photograph of Patton from 1929.[7] Dylan is clearly indulging in racial ambiguity or, put another way, pointing to the possibility of racial capaciousness that he himself can contain.

Dylan has, of course, thought carefully about the politics of race that defines his work, especially the minstrel tradition. *"Love and Theft"* is, again, crucial, since it brings up the issue explicitly. Although Dylan's management has neither confirmed or denied it, the album's title is likely lifted from a book by Eric Lott: *Love and Theft: Blackface Minstrelsy and the American Working Class*. Dylan's title can be read as a description of what his records are all about—lifting lines and tunes from beloved works. But the quotation marks suggest something deeper, perhaps a more direct reference to the content of the book. Lott argues that the expansion of Black minstrelsy in antebellum America was a complex phenomenon of varied significance that went against the dominant reading of the genre as *simply* racist performance tradition meant to belittle and ridicule Black people. He posits that the performance of Blackness, in its initial form, also demonstrated varied audience needs, specifically those of working-class whites in the Northeast (especially New York). Aside from genuine interest in Black performance traditions, blackface provided an outlet for discussing the inequities of society. Audiences, through the act of blackness, could indulge in the show's antiauthoritarian qualities, including its sexually charged elements that bucked the era's sense of propriety. This happened even as racial and class identity hardened by redefining *whiteness* and white superiority in a more expansive way. By gesturing to these sorts of arguments, Dylan acknowledges both the utility and dangers of appropriating the discourses and forms of a multiracial and, indeed, Black musical traditions. Dylan's work is not racist—it is a result of the love part of the equation—but there is a sense that there is another, less pretty, latent, and unintended meaning as well.

The cultural dynamics that first facilitated and rendered possible Dylan's close relationship with Black culture had emerged from a middle-class context, not the working-class one evoked by Lott's narrative. In Grace Hale's extraordinary analysis of the "outsider" in postwar American culture, she emphasizes the category as a middle-class posture, and underlines how the folk revival provided an avenue of youthful rebellion—the effort to reach back and touch premodern days was pointedly in contrast with what was deemed "commercial" and false. By tapping into a wellspring of a prelapsarian world, the emerging (young) counterculture set fetishized the common man and both Black and (poor) white country folk. Black civil rights activists, according to Hale, were happy to play the part of "the folk" to establish rapport and develop support of the white middle class outside of the South. Dylan could not but be a part of this dynamic, a symptom of sorts. Indeed, at a crucial point in his career—the very start—the maneuvering between Black and white culture was a central feature of his success. As Hale puts it, "For a moment, Dylan's art and life made the romance of the outsider seem capacious enough to hold back the conflicts between being black and being white, between being poor and being middleclass, between loving and using the folk."[8] This generosity was articulated or insinuated through performance by taking up the variegated characters or roles associated with a deep historical past, the hobo, the chain gang, etcetera. As mentioned in chapter 2, this is precisely the kind of shape-shifting fundamental to Dylan's initial rise as he placed himself someplace between Guthrie and Johnson, or evoked them each in turn. It was in the interstices of these (racial) types that Dylan could articulate his marginal status.

In practice, of course, Dylan was simply engaging with music he admired. Rock was a genre that did some remarkable racialized work—it ultimately mainstreamed Black cultural/musical materials, making them accessible to white audiences, and subsequently became a (perceived) *white* form of musical expression. Dylan (and others) have never shied away from describing the Black roots of their musical calling, nor has he been one to relegate Black tradition to the role of antecedent; it is not by chance that he often cited the foundational role of Little Richard as a rock star, and thus implicitly supported Richard's own, often strident, assertion of primacy over all rockers that came after him. Of course, Dylan has also aligned himself with white performers who have themselves borrowed from Black styles and sensibilities. Dylan's idolization of Elvis is well known, as is Elvis's time spent on Beale Street picking up what he could from Black blues performers there. Indeed, Elvis's whole stage persona emerges from an entrenched culture of minstrelsy, in form, function, and practice, even if it was not overtly framed as such or even thought of as such by the King.

Dylan enters this world of love and theft from a very particular cultural standpoint. As mentioned already, Dylan has a complicated relationship with Judaism, but there is no doubt that he was raised in a Jewish household and at many points—starting at summer camps and during a brief college stint in a Jewish fraternity—traveled in Jewish circles. I don't want to play the game of trying to establish Dylan's spirituality or his personal religious beliefs—that is his business, and he has kept it mostly guarded for good reason. However, it is worth acknowledging that there is a particular narrative of Jewish and African American interaction in many realms, including music, that cannot be wholly ignored. Jews have been among the most important "translators" of African American forms to broad audiences, and in the early twentieth century notable Jewish men became the most prominent blackface performers. Indeed, Dylan has made direct reference to this tradition.

THE JAZZ SINGER

Al Jolson (born Asa Yoelson) was an immigrant from Lithuania who would become one of the most famous blackface artists of his and any time, immortalized in the movie considered the first talkie, *The Jazz Singer* (1927), the story of the son of a Jewish cantor who cannot accept his son's love for secular music (jazz) and the popular stage.

Dylan has made explicit and implicit mention of Jolson throughout his career. In an interview with Cameron Crowe for the liner notes to *Biograph* (1985) he names Jolson as one of his formative influences, a performer that creates the illusion "that there's a real person talking to me."[9] There is also an obvious reference to Jolson in *Masked and Anonymous* when the blackface performer, Oscar Vogel, appears, as discussed in chapter 1, as an emblem of the origins of Jack Fate's (Dylan) music. Indeed, it is worth noting that "Vogel" means "bird" in German, and Jolson's character in *The Jazz Singer* is Jack Robin.[10]

Elsewhere Dylan points to Jolson's hit movie, which was billed as autobiographical. Dylan references *The Jazz Singer* on the cover of the first edition of his autobiography, *Chronicles*. The image by Don Hunstein is in black-and-white showing Times Square alight with cars whizzing by, the suggestion of pedestrians on the sides, and a lone figure at the center. The sky is pitch dark, absorbing the scene. The image has struck some as an odd choice given that we relate Dylan more with the Village than Broadway. As Marshall Berman has pointed out, however, this is likely a purposeful evocation of *The Jazz Singer*, where at the very end of the film, right when the film's protagonist is about to live out his dream, we see an image of Broadway flanked by lit marquees and Times Square surrounded by a black velvet sky.[11]

Hints at a "shared" biography with Jolson and his persona in *The Jazz Singer* are many, but nowhere more drastically performed that at the 1992 Grammy Awards. After an awful rendition of "Masters of War" and some accolades from Jack Nicholson, Dylan awkwardly received a Lifetime Achievement Award; there was fidgeting, hesitance, and some nervous laughter from the audience, until Dylan finally spits it out. "Well," he said, "my daddy, he didn't leave me much, you know he was a very simple man . . . but what he did tell me was this, he did say, son . . . you know it's possible to become so defiled in this world that your own father and mother will abandon you and if that happens, God will always believe in your ability to mend your ways." Sleuths have traced the language used here to the words of a nineteenth-century rabbi in Germany who said, "Even if I were so depraved that my own mother and father would abandon me to my own devices, God would still gather me up and believe in my ability to mend my ways."[12] The fact that Dylan is borrowing from a rabbi and that it gestures to a paternal warning of defilement, and that the paternal words were retold on the stage of one of music's most important shows and in New York City (Radio City Music Hall) begs and invites a comparisons to Jolson.

Even if the reference is not direct, Dylan is playing with tropes fundamental to *The Jazz Singer*. At core, the film is about the push and pull of tradition and modernity, which plays out in Jolson's character as a man devoted to modern music but tugged at by the traditional cantorial music for which he was groomed to sing. Indeed, the father brutally rejects his son for his modern lusts. At that moment when Jakie Rabinowitz (Jolson) flees from home, the intertitles relay his father's words: "We have no son."

The resonances do not stop there. Although the movie is centered around dichotomies—father/son, sacred/profane music—it is also a meditation on the powers of music itself. Regardless of genre, the movie time and again asserts music's universality, a "rhythm older than civilization." Indeed, there is something godly about it; it emanates from a prime force: "Music is the voice of God." When Jack's (the name he takes on after he leaves home) love interest and theatrical partner, Mary, tries to persuade him to come back to the theater against his parent's pleading, she argues that what they do on the stage is a religion in itself, something Jack had proclaimed in a previous scene: "We in the show business have our religion, too— every day—*the show must go on!*" Things are not quite that simple; Jack ultimately does play cantor for a night, turning his back on Broadway, if momentarily. A scene in which he sings the Kol Nidre is followed by his subsequent arrival on Broadway. As the film suggests, the performer ultimately does not have to choose between the rabbinical and the jazzy, because they are melded through him. Mary, standing at the back of the synagogue, effuses, "The jazz singer, singing to his God." Prior to this, Moishe Yudelson (Warner Oland), on first hearing Jack on stage, links son to father, the worldly to the spiritual: "Just like his Papa—with the cry in his voice." As we've seen already, Dylan has argued that (folk) music is his ultimate religion: "Here's the thing with me and the religious thing. This is the flat-out truth: I find the religiosity and philosophy in the music. I don't find it anywhere else."[13] And as noted above, this musical theology is based not on one strand but on many; borders disappear as something greater is evoked.

The melding described in *The Jazz Singer* is expressly American. When Jack returns home after a long hiatus, he defends his passion for Jazz against his father's disdain: "You're of the old world! If you were born here, you'd feel the same way." Jack's American identity ultimately requires a set of moves, a set of strategies, that both salvages and submerges his Jewishness. Most obviously, his stage name, Jack Robin, erases the "ethnic" resonances of Jakie Rabinowitz. This decision is a practical one within the context of his theatrical aspirations, but it is a deeply personal one as well. It is important that he admonishes his mother that she should refer to him exclusively by his new name. This dynamic is complicated further by the fact that his arrival in showbusiness, the source of his success, is in blackface (and, to an extent, in a Black genre, jazz). When Jack's mother and Moishe see him backstage in his wig and painted features, his mother is taken aback, she doesn't recognize him, and Moishe, also bewildered, says that he "talks like Jakie, but he looks like his shadow." The cantor in him is not gone, but his Americanness is nevertheless possible through suppression of his Jewishness in public, and his absorption of "Blackness." This all clearly resonates with Dylan's history as a performer, from the days that he went from Zimmerman to Dylan in the sixties. Moreover, his embrace of Black musical forms parallels part of the thoroughly American musical persona he has developed over the years.

The close relationship between Blacks and Jews in performance and music is significant for our understanding of Dylan's authorial positioning. Michael Rogin's groundbreaking book *Blackface, White Noise* describes how Jews assimilated African American culture to legitimize their American bona fides at a time when Jews were often seen as outsiders. Jeffrey Melnick, in *A Right to Sing the Blues*, has argued that there is not one "Jewish-Black" relationship and that these complex ties resulted not from inherent affinity but from purposeful work and manipulation. Among other things, he describes how Jewish performers helped mainstream Black musical traditions with the somewhat paradoxical effect of constructing their whiteness.

By habit or happenstance Dylan belongs, at least on the level of morphology, to a long history of Black-Jewish relationships with their manifold valences of loving and borrowing. Dylan is not in the game of performing or establishing racial superiority, but he cannot extricate himself from these narratives of contested power. He is the inheritor of traditions and practices that allow him to assert a white (not Jewish) voice that can be perceived as an embodiment of America itself. As he says in "I Feel a Change Comin' On": "Some people they tell me / I got the blood of the land in my Voice."

CONCLUSION

This chapter has tried to further underline the importance of recombination in Dylan's way of seeing things. The artist himself and the music he performs are constituted by many intermingling traditions and lines of inspiration. But such complexity does not descend into chaos or incomprehension—there is, after all, an artist named Dylan and a musical culture that he considers American. In a way, Dylan subscribes to a melting pot conception of American history. It is a land where different cultural elements can meld into something coherently greater than its parts. If Dylan, in fact, sees things this way, it is not surprising that he is inclined to represent America and its past as culturally coherent despite embedded diversities. Dylan's picture of America and its (musical) traditions can be considered both a result of his analysis of perceived realities—some of which we saw in chapter 3—as well as a manifestation of self-reflection. It is not necessarily the case that Dylan believes himself to represent the totality of a nation or a culture, but it might very well be that he aspires to embody a certain dynamic that he deems fundamental to the American landscape and that he believes can be prominently (and perhaps best) represented through music.

CONCLUSION

When the house lights turn on, when the iPod loses charge, maybe you'll feel a lingering tingle, maybe you'll repeat a line to yourself, maybe you'll hum the bridge. Much later, if the stuff sticks, you'll read a book about the singer or the genre—you might even write one yourself. Music is about the moment—rumination afterward is a fight against the fleeting. We read and write and argue about something fugitive. This book has been an effort to make the music stay, to stamp it, or provide a box where some of Dylan's work might fit.

This project has also been one of self-reflection. Those of us who have chosen to write about Dylan are almost universally admirers. I confess to be among them, though as I say at the start of this book, I cannot be counted among his most fervent followers. I am by trade, as a professional historian, attuned to the historical qualities of Dylan's work. But I also recognize a certain impulse to pull him over to my team. Who, faced with an admired celebrity, doesn't squint and try to see commonality? In light of this, I've fought hard against the self-referential; I've tried to make sure that what I had to say displaced most kinds of fandom. Moreover, I purposefully wrote a book only partially about Dylan; a book that thinks about the past, about how we think about it, how we engage with it, how it is written, and how we perceive it. I'll be the first to admit that there are more obvious paths to these themes.

As I warned from the start, the chapters here do not contain deep analysis of Dylan's songs. This is an art perfected by others, scholar-fans and fan-scholars alike. Instead of treading on those toes, I've wanted to place Dylan within historical traditions and to insist that his work has been, in the fullest sense of the word, historical. To an extent, the reader might be thinking: Duh! But while most attentive listeners intuit historical elements as a secondary or tertiary quality in Dylan's music and words, I wanted to make them coequal with the literary and musical, when appropriate. To do so, this book has focused on historical traditions and modes in hopes that Dylan's work will be more emphatically analyzed within a historiographical framework. Thus, this book does not study the content of the history Dylan writes, but by arguing that historical techniques and impulses permeate aspects of Dylan's work, it follows that his work must have historiographical significance. If the reader accepts this, then it is time to put Dylan's work in conversation with (American) history writ large, to think emphatically about what his work does and does not add to a broader historical conversation. This is something different from saying that Dylan *reflects* an image of America. I want us to engage fully—as Sean Wilentz has started doing—with how his utterances can mingle with other historical versions of America across generic lines.[1]

When it comes to history, Dylan is not unique. We can take the folk tradition whole, we might look at the role of music in historical reenactments, we might consider oldies concerts and tribute bands. In substance and embodiment, we could easily join Dylan to a substantial list of musicians and musical traditions that traffic in what we might call history making. Think, for example, of an artist like Billy Joel, who occasionally evokes past musical traditions and who has written one of the most famous historiographical popular songs, "We Didn't Start the Fire." Think of Amy Winehouse's evocation of retro soul and R&B traditions. Go take a look at Queen Latifah's video for "Ladies First," a song about the empowerment of Black women on a global scale, that incorporates newsreels and collaging techniques. Listen to so many finger-pointing songs, songs of protest that configure and reconfigure hegemonic narratives about the past.[2] Thus, my discussion of Dylan, a musician first, within the context of historiography is an example and an argument for bringing music of all sorts into historical discussions, to take music seriously, not as a cultural artifact that helps write a historical narrative (this, of course, is legitimate and important), but to accept songs (and performances) as historical interventions themselves. Of course, saying that popular forms of history making across many genres and practices should be taken seriously is by no means a new idea. The twist here is that music itself should be taken seriously for its historiographic qualities, something that has only sketchily been done, especially in Western scholarship.

By placing Dylan within various historiographical frameworks, by taking seriously his possible understanding of time and history, by seeing him in historical action, and by touching on how his work has and can be apprehended, I've produced a microhistory, a little slice of modern historical culture. Using Dylan as the focus of such a project requires us to take seriously a realm of history that strays from academic and other stereotypes and that reveals something of the flexibility, the expansiveness, of historical work as it fits in American culture, and perhaps other cultures too.

The past is a playground, but it is a battlefield, too. Performing the past can be a nostalgic kick, but it can also raise a rebel's yell. The very act of reviving ghosts, real and imagined, can function as critique and rebellion.[3] These are paths worth following.

So here are a few questions. What if Dylan is a (great) historian? What then does he, or any musical historian, teach us about the historical craft? Do you, reader, believe that what Dylan says matters within conversations about history? If—and this is not accepted by all—we "traditional" historians are the makers and perpetuators of myths, if we are, as one recent book puts it, "story-tellers, custodians of the past, repositories of collective memory, poetic interpreters of what it is to be human,"[4] why are Dylan's songs rendered purely musical or sometimes poetic while the writerly, often stodgy, words of "proper" historians claim legitimacy and superior import?

If Dylan can stand for a whole world of historical discourse outside of academic halls or the history section at your nearest bookstore, how can we do more to incorporate song and dance into historical discussions, not as primary sources but as historiographical interventions?

Maybe I'll help answer some of these questions sometime somehow, but above all I hope the reader will heed the call—or close this book and (re)listen to "Nettie Moore."[5]

NOTES

INTRODUCTION

1. "Bob Dylan Honored by Gregory Peck with Performance by Dylan," YouTube, accessed January 23, 2018, https://www.youtube.com/watch?v=gixrkvF9xnw.
2. Dan Martin, "Paul Simon: 'I Don't Like Being Second to Bob Dylan,'" *Guardian*, May 12, 2011, https://www.theguardian.com/music/2011/may/12/paul-simon -bob-dylan.
3. Randy Lewis, "Bob Dylan: 'The Homer of Our Time,'" *Los Angeles Times*, October 13, 2016, https://www.latimes.com/entertainment/music/la-et-ms-bob-dylan -nobel-20161013-snap-story.html.
4. "Great Artists Pay Tribute to Their Favorite Bob Dylan Songs," *Rolling Stone Magazine*, May 10, 2011, https://www.rollingstone.com/music/news/great-artists-pay -tribute-to-their-favorite-bob-dylan-songs-20110511.
5. Bob Dylan, "Banquet Speech," NobelPrize.org, accessed January 26, 2018, https://www.nobelprize.org/nobel_prizes/literature/laureates/2016/dylan -speech_en.html.
6. Bob Dylan, "Nobel Lecture," NobelPrize.org, accessed February 12, 2019, https://www.nobelprize.org/prizes/literature/2016/dylan/lecture/.
7. "Press Conference," June 23, 2001, in Jeff Burger, ed., *Dylan on Dylan: Interviews and Encounters* (Chicago, IL: Chicago Press Review, 2018), 404–35 at 410.
8. "Read Bob Dylan's Complete, Riveting MusiCares Speech," *Rolling Stone Magazine*, February 9, 2015, https://www.rollingstone.com/music/news/read-bob-dylans -complete-riveting-musicares-speech-20150209.
9. "Read Bob Dylan's Complete, Riveting MusiCares Speech,"
10. Clinton Heylin, *Behind the Shades: The 20th Anniversary Edition* (London: Faber & Faber, 2011), 726–27.
11. Bob Dylan quoted in Ian Bell, *Once Upon a Time: The Lives of Bob Dylan* (New York: Pegasus Books, 2012), 163.
12. Jonathan Lethem quoted in Burger, *Dylan on Dylan*, 460.
13. Ibid.
14. Sean Wilentz, *Bob Dylan in America* (New York: Doubleday, 2010), 301.
15. Boris Kachka, "Of Thee He Sings: Historian Sean Wilentz Claims Bob Dylan as

One of His own," *New York Magazine*, August 22, 2010, http://nymag.com/guides /fallpreview/2010/books/67621/.

16. Sean Wilentz at the Aspen Institute, Washington, DC, September 2010, YouTube, https://www.youtube.com/watch?v=D5JzaFV6zkA&t=261s (comments begin at about 46:00).

17. Dave Van Ronk quoted in Anthony Scaduto, *Bob Dylan* (New York: Grossett and Dunlap, 1971), 113.

18. For the explicit emphasis on these two realms to the general exclusion of others, see this otherwise beautiful volume: Neil Corcoran, ed. *Do You, Mr. Jones? Bob Dylan with the Poets and Professors* (London: Vintage, 2017). In a sense, this book is trying to do for historicity what Timothy Hampton has done for Dylan's poetics. See Timothy Hampton, *Bob Dylan's Poetics: How the Songs Work* (New York: Zone Books, 2019).

19. See, for example, Roy Rosenzweig and David Thelen, *The Presence of the Past: Popular Uses of History in America Life* (New York: Columbia University Press, 1998), where popular forms of historical representations do not include music.

20. John Michael Runowicz, *Forever Doo-Wop: Race, Nostalgia, and Vocal Harmony* (Amherst: University of Massachusetts Press, 2010).

21. Lise Waxer, *City of Musical Memory: Salsa, Record Grooves, and Popular Culture in Cali, Columbia* (Middletown, CT: Wesleyan University Press, 2002). Matthew Frye Jacobson, *One Grain of Sand* (London: Bloomsbury, 2019).

22. Simon Reynolds, *Retromania: Pop Culture's Addiction to Its Own Past* (New York: Ferrar, Straus, and Giroux, 2011).

23. George Lipsitz, *Time Passages: Collective Memory and American Popular Culture* (Minneapolis: University of Minnesota Press, 1990), 5.

24. Jill Lepore, *The Whites of Their Eyes: The Tea Party's Revolution and the Battle over American History* (Princeton, NJ: Princeton University Press, 2010).

CHAPTER 1: WHAT DO YOU MEAN YOU CAN'T REPEAT THE PAST?

1. Bob Dylan, *Chronicles: Volume One* (New York: Simon and Schuster, 2004), 36.

2. Ibid., 37.

3. Richard F. Thomas, "The Streets of Rome: The Classical Dylan," *Oral Tradition*, 22, no. 1(2007): 30–56 at 41–44. Note, however, that there are some priggish critiques of Dylan's fast and loose treatment of the classics. See, for a particularly annoying example, John Byron Kuhner, "Tangled Up in Thucydides: Bob Dylan Wanes Poetic on Ancient Texts," Eidolon, November 5, 2015, https://eidolon.pub /tangled-up-in-thucydides-7878c4401b8b.

4. Thomas, "Streets of Rome," 42.

5. Jeremy Mynott, ed., *The War of the Peloponnesians and the Athenians* (Cambridge: Cambridge University Press, 2013), 14.

6. Ibid., 15.

7. Ibid.

8. Klaus Meister, "Thucydides in Nineteenth-Century Germany: Historization and Glorification," trans. Neville Morley, in *A Handbook to the Reception of Thucydides*, ed. Christine Lee (New York: John Wiley & Sons, 2015), 197–217.

9. Ibid., 201.

10. Peter Novick, *That Noble Dream, The "Objectivity Question" and the American Historical Profession* (Cambridge: Cambridge University Press, 1988).

11. Lorraine Daston and Peter Galison, *Objectivity* (New York: Zone Books, 2010).

12. Georg G. Iggers, *Historiography in the Twentieth Century: From Scientific Objectivity to the Postmodern Challenge* (Middletown, CT: Wesleyan University Press, 1997), 25.

13. Mynott, *War of the Peloponnesians*, 16.

14. Dylan, *Chronicles*, 89.

15. Quoted in Jeff Burger, ed. *Dylan on Dylan: Interviews and Encounters* (Chicago, IL: Chicago Review Press, 2018), 376.

16. Mynott, *War of the Peloponnesians*, 15.

17. Hayden White, *Metahistory: The Historical Imagination in Nineteenth-Century Europe*, 40th anniversary ed. (Baltimore, MD: The Johns Hopkins University Press, 2014).

18. A good introduction to this in its modern valences is still Joyce Appleby, Lynn Hunt, and Margaret Jacob, *Telling the Truth about History* (New York: Norton, 1994).

19. Umberto Eco, *Confessions of a Young Novelist* (Cambridge, MA: Harvard University Press, 2011), 110–19.

20. Dylan, *Chronicles*, 35.

21. Mynott, *War of the Peloponnesians*, 110.

22. Ibid., 114.

23. Ibid., 212.

24. Ibid.

25. Dylan, *Chronicles*, 35.

26. Toby Creswell, "Gates of Eden Revisited: A Conversation with Bob Dylan (1986)," in *Younger Than That Now: The Collected Interviews with Bob Dylan*, ed. Jim Ellison (New York: Da Capo Press, 2004), 244.

27. Mikal Gilmore, "Bob Dylan Unleashed," *Rolling Stone Magazine*, September 27, 2012, https://www.rollingstone.com/music/music-news/bob-dylan-unleashed-189723/.

28. Here Dylan is likely thinking about these historical practitioners as described by Tony Horwitz, *Confederates in the Attic: Dispatches from the Unfinished Civil War* (New York: Vintage, 1998). This book's title is based on Horwitz's book as well.

29. Ibid.

30. Robert Fagles, ed., *The Odyssey* (New York: Penguin, 1999), 194.

31. François Hartog, *Regimes of Historicity: Presentism and Experiences of Time* (New York: Columbia University Press, 2015), 51–52.

32. Bob Dylan, *Nobel Lecture*, June 5, 2017, https://www.nobelprize.org/prizes/literature/2016/dylan/lecture/.

33. Mikal Gilmore, "Bob Dylan on His Dark New Album, 'Tempest,'" *Rolling Stone*, August 1, 2012, https://www.rollingstone.com/music/music-news/bob-dylan-on-his-dark-new-album-tempest-184271/.

34. [Andrea Svedberg], "I Am My Words," *Newsweek*, November 4, 1963.

35. Excerpt from Izzy Young's journal, October 20, 1961, quoted in Scott Barretta, ed., *The Conscience of the Folk Revival: The Writings of Israel "Izzy" Young* (Lanham, MD: Scarecrow Press, 2013), 23. Young reads this bit from his journals in *No Direction Home*, dir. Martin Scorsese, DVD (Burbank, CA: Paramount Pictures, 2005).

36. A charming animated video of the interview can be found at Kory Grow, "See 20-Year-Old Bob Dylan Talk Early Carnival Life in Animated Interview," *Rolling*

Stone, June 28, 2016, https://www.rollingstone.com/music/music-news/see-20 -year-old-bob-dylan-talk-early-carnival-life-in-animated-interview-119180/.

37. Bob Dylan quoted in Sean Wilentz, *Bob Dylan in America* (New York: Doubleday, 2010), 169. A good survey of carnival speak and Dylan is Scott Warmuth, swarmuth.blogspot, April 17, 2009, https://swarmuth.blogspot.com/2009/04 /together-through-life-dispatch-7.html.

38. Ibid.

39. Rachel Adams, *Sideshow USA: Freaks and the American Cultural Imagination* (Chicago, IL: University of Chicago Press, 2001), 60–88.

40. Sergei Petrov and Rene Fontaine [Dylan and Charles], *Masked and Anonymous*, draft, March 21, 2002, 54, https://archive.org/details/masked-and-anonymous-screen play-revised-draft-5-21-02.

41. P. T. Barnum, *The Life of P. T. Barnum* (London: Sampson Low, Son, 1855), 149.

42. Joice Heth advertisement, *New York Sun*, August 21, 1835, https://lostmuseum.cuny. edu/archive/joice-heth-advertisement-new-york-sun-august.

43. Kevin Young, *Bunk: The Rise of Hoaxes, Humbug, Plagiarists, Phonies, Post-Facts, and Fake News* (Minneapolis, MN: Greywolf Press, 2017), 36.

44. Marc Hartzman, *American Sideshow: An Encyclopedia of History's most Wondrous and Curiously Strange Performers* (New York: Penguin, 2005).

45. Lorraine Daston and Katharine Park, *Wonders and the Order of Nature, 1150–1750* (New York: Zone Books, 2001).

46. "A Foreign Graudec in Philadelphia," *Morning Herald*, November 22, 1837.

47. Sianne Ngai, *Theory of the Gimmick: Aesthetic Judgement and Capitalist Form* (Cambridge, MA: Harvard University Press, 2020)

48. Barnum, *Life*, 148.

49. Wilentz, *Bob Dylan in America*, 169.

50. Dylan, *Chronicles*, 234.

51. Petrov and Fontaine, *Masked and Anonymous*, 110.

52. David Yaffe, *Bob Dylan: Like a Complete Unknown* (New Haven, CT: Yale University Press, 2011), 60.

53. Interviews from Martin Scorsese, *No Direction Home*, track 6, CD accompanying Robert Santelli, *The Bob Dylan Scrapbook, 1956–1966* (New York: Simon and Schuster, 2005).

54. John Szwed, *Alan Lomax: The Man Who Recorded the World* (New York: Viking, 2010).

55. Philip V. Bohlman, *Song Loves the Masses: Herder on Music and Nationalism* (Berkeley: University of California Press, 2017), 29.

56. Esther K. Birdsall, "Some Notes on the Role of George Lyman Kittredge in American Folklore Studies," *Journal of the Folklore Institute* 10, no. 1/2 (1973): 57–66.

57. Sean O'Neill, "The Boasian Legacy in Ethonomusicology: Cultural Relativism, Narrative Texts, Linguistic Structures, and the Role of Comparison," in *The Franz Boas Papers*, vol. 1, *Franz Boas as Public Intellectual—Theory, Ethnography, Activism*, ed. Regna Darnell, Michelle Hamilton, Robert L. A. Hancock, and Joshua Smith (Omaha: University of Nebraska Press, 2015), 129–62 at 147.

58. George W. Stocking, "Introduction: The Basic Assumptions of Boasian Anthropology," in *A Franz Boas Reader: The Shaping of American Anthropology, 1883–1911* (Chicago, IL: University of Chicago Press, 1974), 12–15.

59. Quoted in Szwed, *Lomax*, 85.

60. Paul Allen Anderson, *Deep River: Music and Memory in Harlem Renaissance Thought* (Durham, NC: Duke University Press), esp. 167–218.

61. Nolan Porterfield, *Last Cavalier: The Life and Times of John A. Lomax, 1867–1948* (Urbana: University of Illinois Press, 1996), 121.

62. Alan Lomax, *The Land Where the Blues Began* (New York: Delta, 1993), 4.

63. Dylan, *Chronicles*, 29.

64. Ibid., 35.

65. Ibid., 46–47.

66. Ibid., 47.

67. "Still on the Road: 1961 Concerts and Recording Sessions," bjorner.com, February 8, 2022, https://www.bjorner.com/DSN00020%201961.htm.

68. "Robbie Robertson Talks about Bob Dylan and the Basement Tapes," YouTube, May 31, 2022, https://www.youtube.com/watch?v=1lD-64YsRgo.

69. John Hay, "Theme Time: Bob Dylan as DJ," in *New Approaches*, ed. Anne-Marie Mai (Odense: University Press of Southern Denmark, 2019), 191.

70. Scott M. Marshall, *Bob Dylan: A Spiritual Life* (Washington, DC: BP Books / WND Books, 2017), 11.

71. Timothy Hampton, *Bob Dylan's Poetics: How the Songs Work* (Brooklyn, NY: Zone Books, 2019), 179–81.

72. Bob Dylan in Syracuse, May 1980, quoted in Clinton Heylin, ed., *Saved! The Gospel Speeches* (Madras: Hanuman Books, 1990), 9.

73. Bob Dylan in San Diego, November 1978, quoted in Heylin, *Saved!*, 8.

74. Andrew McCarron, *Light Come Shining: The Transformations of Bob Dylan* (Oxford: Oxford University Press, 2017), 80.

75. Hal Lindsey with C. C. Carlson, *The Late Great Planet Earth* (1970; repr., Grand Rapids, MI: Zodervan, 1980). Hal Lindsey with C. C. Carlson, *Satan Is Alive and Well on Planet Earth* (Grand Rapids, MI: Zodervan, 1972).

76. Lindsey, *Planet Earth*, 55.

77. Ibid., 57.

78. Bob Dylan in Albuquerque, December 5, 1979, quoted in Heylin, *Saved!*, 13.

79. Bob Dylan in Toronto, April 20, 1980, quoted in Heylin, *Saved!*, 15–17.

80. Bob Dylan in San Francisco, November 16, 1979, quoted in Heylin, *Saved!*, 22.

81. Bob Dylan in San Francisco November 26, 1979, quoted in Heylin, *Saved!*, 44.

82. David E. Kaufman, *Jewhooing the Sixties: American Celebrity and Jewish Identity* (Waltham, MA: Brandeis University Press, 2012), 155–212. Louie Kemp, *Dylan and Me: 50 Years of Adventures* (Los Angeles, CA: Westrose Press, 2019)

83. Rabbi Meir Kahane, *The Story of the Jewish Defense League* (Randor, PA: Chilton, 1975).

84. Images available as part of auction lot "#5032—Bob Dylan Hand-Annotated 1971 Interview Transcript (Tape #2, First Correction)" at RR Auction, accessed October 30, 2020. https://www.rrauction.com/preview_itemdetail.cfm?IN=5032. Also consulted was Mathilde Frot, "Bob Dylan Offers Rare Glimpse into His Jewish Identity in Previously Unpublished Interview," JC.com, October 28, 2020, https://www.thejc.com/news/world/bob-dylan-offers-rare-glimpse-into-his-jewish-identity-in-previously-unpublished-interview-1.507966. Accessed 10/30/20.

85. Susan Neiman, *Learning from the Germans: Race and Memory of Evil* (New York: FSG, 2020), 26–27.

86. Kaufman, *Jewhooing the Sixties*, 155–212.
87. Britta Lee Shain, *Seeing the Real You at Last: Life and Love on the Road with Bob Dylan* (London: Jawbone Press, 2016), 192.
88. Bob Dylan, *Tarantula* (New York: Scribner, 2004), 54.
89. Seth Rogovy, *Bob Dylan: Prophet, Mystic, Poet* (New York: Scribner, 2009), 142.
90. Dylan, *Chronicles*, 28–29.
91. Mikal Gilmore, "Bob Dylan Unleashed," *Rolling Stone,* September 27, 2012, https://www.rollingstone.com/music/music-news/bob-dylan-unleashed-189723/.
92. See https://www.greatpassionplay.org/.
93. Dylan, *Chronicles*, 128.
94. John Baudlie, ed., *Wanted Man: In Search of Bob Dylan* (New York: Citadel Press, 1990), 73.
95. David Segal, "Knockin' on Dylan's Door," *Washington Post*, August 31, 2003, https://www.washingtonpost.com/archive/lifestyle/style/2003/08/31/knockin-on-dylans-door/e7c7e1f2-dbc1-4e03-8621-c1993ce9ca3b/.
96. Bob Dylan quoted in Murray Leeder, "Haunting and Minstrelsy in Bob Dylan's Masked and Anonymous," *Journal of Popular Film and Television* 40, no. 4 (2012): 182.
97. Molly McGarry, *Ghosts of Future Pasts: Spiritualism and the Cultural Politics of Nineteenth-Century America* (Berkeley: University of California Press, 2008), 8.
98. "Dylan Unnoticed on Beatles Tour," BBC News Channel, May 12, 2009, https://news.bbc.co.uk/2/hi/uk_news/england/merseyside/8046278.stm.
99. Andy Greene, "Bob Dylan Makes Pilgrimage to Neil Young's Childhood Home," *Rolling Stone*, November 11, 2008, https://www.rollingstone.com/music/music-news/bob-dylan-makes-pilgrimage-to-neil-youngs-childhood-home-102566/.
100. Richard Lang, "The Dwelling Door," in *Dwelling, Place, and Environment*, ed. D. Seamon and R. Mugerauer (Dordrecht: Martinus Nijhoff, 1985), 202.
101. Bruce Conforth and Gayle Dean Wardlow, *Up Jumped the Devil: The Real Life of Robert Johnson* (Chicago, IL: Chicago Review Press, 2019), 104–5.
102. Mikal Gilmore. "Bob Dylan Unleashed," *Rolling Stone*, September 27, 2012, https://www.rollingstone.com/music/music-news/bob-dylan-unleashed-189723/.
103. Dylan, *Chronicles*, 79.
104. Benedict XVI, *Angelus*, Castel Gandolfo, August 6, 2006, http://w2.vatican.va/content/benedict-xvi/en/angelus/2006/documents/hf_ben-xvi_ang_20060806.html.
105. *Catechism of the Catholic Church*, chapter 2, article 3, paragraph 3, no. 555, Vatican.va, accessed May 31, 2022, https://www.vatican.va/archive/ENG0015/__P1L.HTM.
106. McCarron, *Light Come Shining*, 56.
107. Copyright © Bob Dylan 2022. "'Jimi—written for The Jimi Hendrix Exhibition by Alan Douglass at Govinda Gallery in 1993, copyright 1998," from Box 96, Folder 5, of The Bob Dylan Archive® collections, American Song Archives, Tulsa, OK, courtesy of the George Kaiser Family Foundation.
108. "Album of the Year," Youtube.com, accessed May 29, 2022, https://www.youtube.com/watch?v=sChR4I-mOSM.
109. Elizabeth Hellmuth Margulis, *On Repeat: How Music Plays the Mind* (Oxford: Oxford University Press, 2014); Patrick N. Juslin, "Emotional Reactions to Music" in *The Oxford Handbook of Music Psychology*, ed. Susan Hallam, Ian Cross, and Michael

Thaut, 2nd ed. (Oxford: Oxford University Press, 2016), 197–214; David Clarke and Eric Clarke, eds., *Music and Consciousness: Philosophical, Psychological, and Cultural Perspectives* (Oxford: Oxford University Press, 2011).

110. Ian Bostridge, *Schubert's Winter Journey: Anatomy of an Obsession* (New York: Knopf, 2015), 99.

111. John Butt, *Playing with History: The Historical Approach to Musical Performance* (Cambridge: Cambridge University Press, 2002); Richard Taruskin, *Text and Act: Essays on Music and Performance* (Oxford: Oxford University Press, 1995).

112. Robert Cantwell, *When We Were Good: The Folk Revival* (Cambridge, MA: Harvard University Press, 1997).

113. *Broadside*, no. 1 (February 1962): n.p.

114. Matthew Gelbart, *The Invention of "Folk Music" and "Art Music": Emerging Categories from Ossian to Wagner* (Cambridge: Cambridge University Press, 2007), 162.

115. Szwed, *Lomax*, 38.

116. A good deal of scholarship has explored the ambiguities of Lomax's project as it relates to race and power dynamics. See, for example, Patrick B. Mullen, *The Man Who Adores the Negro: Race and American Folklore* (Urbana: University of Illinois Press, 2008), esp. 79–116. Lomax's work as compared with other song collectors has recently received a rich treatment in Steven Garabedian, *A Sound History: Lawrence Gellert, Black Musical Protest, and White Denial* (Amherst: University of Massachusetts Press, 2020), esp. 81–107.

117. Scott Barretta, ed., *Conscience of the Folk Revival: The Writings of Israel "Izzy" Young* (Lanhan, MD: Scarecrow Press, 2013), 42.

118. Thanks to Richard Sonn for letting me borrow this story. On the song, see Megan Garber, "Ashokan Farewell: The Story behind the Tune Ken Burns made Famous," *Atlantic*, September 25, 2015, https://www.theatlantic.com/entertainment/archive/2015/09/ashokan-farewell-how-a-20th-century-melody-became-an-anthem-for-the-19th/407263/.

119. "No Direction Home Outtakes," in Burger, *Dylan on Dylan*, 399

120. Stephen Halliwell, *The Aesthetics of Mimesis: Ancient Texts and Modern Problems* (Princeton, NJ: Princeton University Press, 2002), 21.

121. Stephen Wade, *The Beautiful Music All around Us: Field Recordings and American Experience* (Urbana, Ill. University of Illinois Press, 2012), 36.

122. Mikal Gilmore, "Dylan Unleashed," *Rolling Stone*, September 27, 2012, https://www.rollingstone.com/music/music-news/bob-dylan-unleashed-189723/.

123. Boris Kachka, "Of Thee He Sings: Historian Sean Wilentz Claims Bob Dylan as One of His Own," *New York Magazine*, August 22, 2010, http://nymag.com/guides/fallpreview/2010/books/67621/.

CHAPTER 2: "CONJURING UP ALL THESE LONG DEAD SOULS"

1. "Larry Charles' 'Bob Dylan Slapstick-Comedy' Story," November 25, 2020, https://www.youtube.com/watch?v=JQDTSu8v8QI.

2. Such a hardline understanding was embraced by many, including, for example,

Dave Van Ronk; see Dave Van Ronk with Elijah Wald, *Mayor of MacDougal Street: A Memoir* (Cambridge, MA: Da Capo Press, 2006), 27.

3. Steven Rings, "A Foreign Sound to Your Ear: Bob Dylan Performs 'It's Alright, Ma (I'm Only Bleeding),' 1964–2009," *MTO* 19, no. 4 (December 2013): Section 16.

4. Thomas Crow, *The Long March of Pop: Art, Music, and Design, 1930–1995* (New Haven, CT: Yale University Press, 2014). 3.

5. Ibid.

6. Ibid., 50. For these trends in contemporary art, see Toby Kamps, *The Old, Weird America: Folk Themes in Contemporary Art* (Houston, TX: Contemporary Arts Museum, 2008).

7. *Revisionist Art: Thirty Works by Bob Dylan* (New York: Abrams, 2012).

8. "Bob Dylan: The Asia Series," Gagosian.com, December 5, 2020, https://gagosian.com/exhibitions/2011/bob-dylan-the-asia-series/.

9. "Bob Dylan Explains a Writing Technique—'Don't Look Back' Outtake, 1965," YouTube, accessed May 27, 2022, https://www.youtube.com/watch?v=TpRqHc-TC8g.

10. T. S. Eliot, "Tradition and the Individual Talent," in *The Sacred Wood: Essays on Poetry and Criticism*, by T. S. Eliot (New York: Knopf, 1921), 42–54 at 49.

11. Ibid., 44.

12. Andrea Cossu, *It Ain't Me, Babe: Bob Dylan and the Performance of Authenticity* (New York: Routledge, 2012); Lee Marshall, *Bob Dylan: The Never Ending Star* (London: Polity, 2013).

13. For a useful and theorized discussion of authorship and related issues, see Anne-Marie Mai, *Bob Dylan: The Poet* (Odense: University Press of Southern Denmark, 2018), 25–35.

14. Paul Williams, *Bob Dylan Performing Artist: The Early Years, 1960–1973* (1991; repr., London: Omnibus Press, 2004), xiv

15. Douglas Brinkley, "Inside Bob Dylan's Lost Interviews and Unseen Letters," *Rolling Stone*, October 21, 2020, https://www.rollingstone.com/music/music-features/bob-dylan-lost-letters-interviews-tony-glover-1074916/.

16. Bob Dylan, *Chronicles: Volume One* (New York: Simon and Schuster, 2004), 122.

17. Joe Levy, "Inside Bob Dylan's 'Time Out of Mind' Sessions," *Rolling Stone*, September 30, 2017, https://www.rollingstone.com/music/music-features/inside-bob-dylans-time-out-of-mind-sessions-200926/.

18. William Fowlie and Seth Whidden, eds., *Rimbaud: Complete Works, Selected Letters* (Chicago, IL: University of Chicago Press, 2005), 370–71.

19. Ian Bell, *Time Out of Mind: The Lives of Bob Dylan* (New York: Pegasus Books, 2013), 303.

20. "Bob Dylan FULL 60 Minutes Ed Bradley 2004 Interview," YouTube, accessed May 27, 2022, https://www.youtube.com/watch?v=hOasod-fFK8.

21. Jonathan Lethem, "The Genius and Modern Times of Bob Dylan," *Rolling Stone*, September 7, 2006, https://www.rollingstone.com/feature/the-genius-and-modern-times-of-bob-dylan-237203/.

22. Rebecca Schneider, *Theatre and History* (London: Springer, 2014), 65.

23. For an important early study along these lines, see Betsy Bowden, *Performed Literature: Words and Music by Bob Dylan* (Bloomington: Indiana University Press, 1982). Most

recently, see Keith Nainby and John Radosta, *Bob Dylan in Performance: Song, Stage, and Screen* (Washington, DC: Lexington Books, 2019).

24. Quoted in David Weiss, "You're 100 Per cent Wrong About Bob Dylan," *Newsweek*, July 5, 2015, https://www.newsweek.com/2015/07/17/youre-100-wrong-about -bob-dylan-349964.html.

25. Copyright © Bob Dylan 2022. "Draft of Stevie Wonder Rock and Roll Hall of Fame induction speech (1989)," Box 96, Folder 06, Item 01, of The Bob Dylan Archive® collections, American Song Archives, Tulsa, OK, courtesy of the George Kaiser Family Foundation.

26. Jonathan Cott, *Bob Dylan: The Essential Interviews* (New York: Werner Books, 2006), 227.

27. David Yaffe, *Bob Dylan: Like a Complete Unknown* (New Haven, CT: Yale University Press, 2011), 5.

28. Robert Shelton, "Bob Dylan: A Distinctive Folk-Song Stylist," *New York Times*, September 29, 1961, L31.

29. "Bob Dylan Hand-Annotated 1971 Interview Transcript (Day #3, First Correction)," ComeWritersandCritics.com, accessed December 27, 2020, page 3, https:// www.bobdylan-comewritersandcritics.com/largeimages/odds/tony-glover-1971 -interview/1971-03-24-glover-interview-1st-correction-3.jpg.

30. Steven Rings, "Here's Your Throat Back, Thanks for the Loan: On Bob Dylan's Voices," lecture at the University of Chicago in 2012, posted March 26, 2015, https://alldylan.com/steven-rings-heres-your-throat-back-thanks-for-the-loan- on-dylans-voices-video/.

31. LeRoi Jones, *Blues People: Negro Music in White America* (1969; repr., New York: Quill, 1999), 29.

32. Jennifer Lynn Stoever, *The Sonic Color Line: Race and the Cultural Politics of Listening* (New York: New York University Press, 2016), 201.

33. Robert Love, "Bob Dylan: The Uncut Interview," in *Dylan on Dylan: Interviews and Encounters*, ed. Jeff Burger (Chicago, IL: Chicago Review Press, 2018), 492.

34. Ibid., 504.

35. For a trailblazing take on Dylan's body, see Ann Powers, "Gender and Sexuality: Bob Dylan's Body," in *The World of Bob Dylan*, ed. Sean Latham (Cambridge: Cambridge University Press, 2021), 264–77.

36. Robert Shelton, "Bob Dylan: A Distinctive Folk-Song Stylist," *New York Times*, September 29, 1961, L31; Robert Shelton "Bob Dylan Sings His Compositions," *New York Times*, Saturday, April 13, 1963, L 11.

37. Larry Sloman, *On the Road with Bob Dylan* (New York: Crown, 2002), 200.

38. Ann Powers, *Good Booty: Love and Sex, Black and White, Body and Soul in American Music* (New York: Dey Street, 2017).

39. "Bob Dylan—Once Upon a Time—Tony Bennett Celebrates 90 12/20/16," YouTube, February 13, 2022, https://www.youtube.com/watch?v=qPAE1hZ4fxc.

40. Greil Marcus, *Three Songs, Three Singers, Three Nations* (Cambridge, MA: Harvard University Press, 2015), 1–13.

41. Sean Latham, "Roadhouse on the River Styx," University of Tulsa, July 20, 2021. https://dylan.utulsa.edu/roadhouse-on-the-river-styx/.

42. Jon Pareles, "Releases from Bob Dylan and Diana Krall," *New York Times*, February

2, 2015, https://www.nytimes.com/2015/02/03/arts/music/releases-from-bob
-dylan-and-diana-krall.html?_r=0.

43. Koji Matsudo, "Time Out of Mind as Distant Past beyond Memory: Bob Dylan
and His 'Late Style'" (master's thesis, City College of the City University of New
York, 2011), 27–28.

44. Ibid., 28.

45. Copyright © Bob Dylan 2022. Miscellaneous notes from World Gone Wrong, circa.
1993, Box 94, Folder 6, of The Bob Dylan Archive® collections, American Song
Archives, Tulsa, OK, courtesy of the George Kaiser Family Foundation.

46. John Hay, "Theme Time: Bob Dylan as DJ," in Mai, *New Approaches*, 189–203 at
191.

47. Ibid.

48. *Theme Time Radio Hour*, episode 82: "Fruit," https://www.themetimeradio.com
/episode-82-fruit/.

49. Bell, *Time Out of Mind*, 244–45.

CHAPTER 3: "SING IN ME, OH MUSES"

1. Joseph Mali, *Mythistory: The Making of a Modern Historiography* (Chicago, IL: University of Chicago Press, 2003), 11.

2. Greil Marcus, *Three Songs, Three Singers, Three Nations* (Cambridge, MA: Harvard
University Press, 2015), 83.

3. Bob Dylan, *Chronicles: Volume One* (New York: Simon and Schuster, 2004), 39.

4. Quoted in David Dalton, *Who Is That Man? In Search of the Real Bob Dylan* (New
York: Omnibus, 2012).

5. Bob Dylan, "World Gone Wrong," BobDylan.com, February 11, 2022, https://
www.bobdylan.com/albums/world-gone-wrong/.

6. Christopher Ricks, *Dylan's Vision of Sin* (New York: Ecco, 2005).

7. David Kiney, *The Dylanologists: Adventures in the Land of Bob* (New York: Simon &
Schuster, 2014), 129.

8. Bob Dylan, "The Ballad of Hollis Brown," disc 1, track 15 on *The Bootleg Series*, vol.
9, *The Witmark Demos: 1962–1964*, Columbia Records, CD.

9. Gilmore, "Bob Dylan on His Dark New Album," *Rolling Stone*, accessed December
1, 2020, https://www.rollingstone.com/music/music-news/bob-dylan-on-his-dark
-new-album-tempest-184271/.

10. Ibid.

11. Christina Sharpe, *In the Wake: On Blackness and Being* (Durham, NC: Duke University
Press, 2017).

12. Exodus 12:7 (King James Version).

13. Ian Bell, *Time Out of Mind: The Lives of Bob Dylan* (New York: Pegasus Books, 2013),
452.

14. "Bob Dylan and the NECLC," Corliss-Lamont.org, accessed February 14, 2022,
https://www.corliss-lamont.org/dylan.htm.

15. Christopher Ricks, Lisa Nemrow, and Julie Nemrow, eds., *The Lyrics* (New York:
Simon and Schuster, 2014), 888.

16. Email exchange with Christopher Ricks, December 9, 2020.

17. Dylan, *Chronicles*, 86.

18. Ibid., 74.

19. Ibid., 84.

20. Ibid.

21. Mikal Gilmore, "Bob Dylan Unleashed," *Rolling Stone*, September 27, 2012, https://www.rollingstone.com/music/music-news/bob-dylan-unleashed-189723/.

22. Ibid.

23. "Bob Dylan and the NECLC," Corliss-Lamont.org, accessed February 14, 2022, https://www.corliss-lamont.org/dylan.htm.

24. Bob Dylan, "Blind Willie McTell," BobDylan.com, January 16, 2022, https://www.bobdylan.com/songs/blind-willie-mctell/.

25. Mike Marqusee, *Wicked Messenger: Bob Dylan and the 1960s* (New York: Seven Stories Press, 2005), 87.

CHAPTER 4: THERE'S SOMETHING HAPPENING HERE . . . MR. JONES"

1. Dave Marsh, "Review of *Desire*," March 11, 1976, *Rolling Stone*, https://www.rollingstone.com/music/music-album-reviews/desire-255500/.

2. "The Hurricane Tapes," BBC, February 9, 2022, https://www.bbc.co.uk/programmes/w13xttt6/episodes/downloads.

3. Sarah Larson, "'The Hurricane Tapes': Will a British Podcast Solve the Hurricane Carter Case?," *New Yorker*, March 13, 2019, https://www.newyorker.com/culture/podcast-dept/the-hurricane-tapes-will-a-british-podcast-solve-the-hurricane-carter-case.

4. Howard Sounes, *Down the Highway: The Life of Bob Dylan* (New York: Grove Press, 2001), 133.

5. Ibid.

6. Sean Wilentz, *Bob Dylan in America* (New York: Doubleday, 2010), 8.

7. Ibid., 232.

8. Daniel Wolff, *Grown-Up Anger: The Connected Mysteries of Bob Dylan, Woodie Guthrie, and the Calumet Massacre of 1913* (New York: Harper Collins, 2017), 18.

9. Matthew Frye Jacobson, *The Historian's Eye: Photography, History, and the American Present* (Chapel Hill: The University of North Carolina Press, 2019), 5.

10. Mikal Gilmore, "Bob Dylan Unleashed," *Rolling Stone*, September 27, 2012, https://www.rollingstone.com/music/music-news/bob-dylan-unleashed-189723/.

11. Richard Thomas, *Why Bob Dylan Matters* (New York: Dey Street Books), 167.

12. Ibid., 254.

13. Ibid., 259.

14. Ibid., 262.

15. Ibid., 265.

16. Jeff Burger, ed., *Dylan on Dylan: Interviews and Encounters* (Chicago, IL: Chicago Press Review, 2018), 460.

17. Wilentz, *Dylan in America*, 13.

18. Ibid., 12.

19. Greil Marcus, *Three Songs, Three Singers, Three Nations* (Cambridge, MA: Harvard University Press, 2015), 45.

20. Greil Marcus, *Bob Dylan by Greil Marcus: Writings, 1968–2010* (New York: Public Affairs, 2010), 157.

21. Ibid.

22. Ibid., 160.

23. Jean-Martin Büttner, "Greil Marcus and Bob Dylan: The Writer and His Singer," in *Refractions of Bob Dylan: Cultural Appropriations of an American Icon*, ed. Eugen Banauch (Manchester, UK: Manchester University Press, 2015), 135–46 at 137.

24. Marcus, *Three Songs*, 44–45.

25. Ibid., 46.

26. Ibid., 48.

27. Greil Marcus, *Mystery Train: Images of America in Rock 'n' Roll Music* (New York: Penguin, 2015), 115.

28. Greil Marcus, "Images of the Present Day," in *Double Trouble: Bill Clinton and Elvis Presley in the Land of No Alternatives*, by Greil Marcus (New York: Picador), 26–27.

29. Greil Marcus and Sean Wilentz, eds., *The Rose and the Briar: Death, Love, and Liberty in the American Ballad* (New York: W. W. Norton, 2005), 1.

30. I take "Dylan Town" from David Gaines, *In Dylan Town: A Fan's Life* (Iowa City: University of Iowa Press, 2015).

31. Greil Marcus, *The Old, Weird America: The World of Bob Dylan's Basement Tapes*, 2nd ed. (New York: Picador, 2011), 189.

32. Ibid., 190.

33. Greil Marcus, *Like a Rolling Stone: Bob Dylan at the Crossroads: An Explosion of Vision and Humor That Forever Changed Pop Music* (New York: Public Affairs, 2005), 201.

34. John Lomax, "Collector's Note" in *Cowboy Songs and Other Frontier Ballads*, ed. John Lomax (New York: Macmillan, 1922), n.p.

35. Description taken from the title of Brinkley's article, "Bob Dylan's Late-Era, Old-Style American Individualism," *Rolling Stone*, May 14, 2009, https://www .rollingstone.com/music/music-news/bob-dylans-late-era-old-style-american-in dividualism-90298/.

36. Ann Powers, "To Capture Bob Dylan's Rolling Thunder Revue, Martin Scorsese Had to Get Weird," NPR, June 10, 2019, https://www.npr.org/2019/06/10/731305441 /to-capture-bob-dylans-rolling-thunder-revue-martin-scorsese-had-to-get -weird.

37. The lies have been listed by many at this point. See David Ehlrish, Chris O'Falt, and Zack Sharp, "Debunking the Four Big Lies at the Heart of Martin Scorsese's 'Rolling Thuder Revue,'" *IndieWire*, June 12, 2019, https://www.indiewire. com/2019/06/rolling-thunder-revue-secrets-scorsese-dylan-netflix-1202149452/. Larry Fitzmaurice, "What Is Fact and What Is Fiction in Martin Scorsese's Rolling Thunder Revue: A Bob Dylan Story," *Vulture*, June 13, 2019, https://www.vulture. com/2019/06/rolling-thunder-revue-what-is-true-and-what-is-fake.html.

CHAPTER 5: "THE BLOOD OF THE LAND
IN MY VOICE"

1. Douglas Brinkley, "Bob Dylan Has a Lot on His Mind," *New York Times*, June 12, 2020, https://www.nytimes.com/2020/06/12/arts/music/bob-dylan-rough-and-rowdy-ways.html?searchResultPosition=1.

2. "Bob Dylan Hand-Annotated 1971 Interview Transcript (Tape #2, First

Correction)," ComeWritersandCritics.com, accessed December 27, 2020, page 2, https://www.bobdylan-comewritersandcritics.com/largeimages/odds/tony-glover-1971-interview/glover-1971-interview-2.jpg.

3. See, for example, Jack Hamilton, *Just Around Midnight: Rock and Roll and the Racial Imagination* (Cambridge, MA: Harvard University Press, 2016).

4. Guthrie Ramsey, *Race Music: Black Cultures from Bebop to Hips-Hop* (Berkeley: University of California Press, 2003).

5. Ben Wynne, *In Tune: Charley Patton, Jimmie Rodgers, and the Roots of American Music* (Baton Rouge: Louisiana State University Press, 2014), 63–66; David Evans, "Charley Patton: The Conscience of the Delta," in *Charley Patton: Voice of the Mississippi Delta*, ed. Robert Sacré (Jackson: University Press of Mississippi, 2018), 23–138.

6. Wynne, *In Tune*, 63.

7. Greil Marcus, *Bob Dylan by Greil Marcus: Writings, 1968–2010* (New York: Public Affairs, 2010), 385.

8. Grace Elizabeth Hale, *A Nation of Outsiders: How the White Middle Class Fell in Love with Rebellion in Postwar America* (Oxford: Oxford University Press, 2011), 87.

9. Interview with Cameron Crowe in liner notes to *Biograph* (Columbia Records, 1985), 25.

10. Thanks to Jeff Melnick for pointing this out.

11. Marshall Berman, "Broadway, Love, and Theft: Al Jolson's *Jazz Singer*," in *Modernism in the Streets: A Life and Times in Essays*, by Marshall Berman (New York: Verso, 2017).

12. Martin Grossman post on rec.music.dylan, August 10, 1998, in "Bob Dylan's Grammy Speech 1991," Expectingrain.com, accessed May 22, 2022, https://www.expectingrain.com/dok/int/grammiesspeech.html.

13. David Gates, "Dylan Revisited," *Newsweek*, October, 5, 1997, https://www.newsweek.com/dylan-revisited-174056.

CONCLUSION

1. To my knowledge, only Sean Wilentz has started doing the historiographical work that I encourage here. See his masterful essay "Bob Dylan, Historian," *New York Review of Books*, June 19, 2021, https://www.nybooks.com/daily/2021/06/19/bob-dylan-historian/?lp_txn_id=1323049.

2. For some insightful clues about this, though now almost thirty years old, see George Lipsitz, *Dangerous Crossroads: Popular Music, Postmodernism, and the Poetics of Space* (New York: Verso, 1994).

3. See, for example, Rachel Lee Rubin, *Well Met: Renaissance Faires and the American Counterculture* (New York: New York University Press, 2012).

4. Priya Satia, *Time's Monster: How History Makes History* (Cambridge, MA: Harvard University Press, 2020), 1.

5. Reference to this song is by way of Robert Reginio, "'Nettie Moore': Minstrelsy and the Cultural Economy of Race in Bob Dylan's Late Albums," in *Highway 61 Revisited: Bob Dylan's Road from Minnesota to the World*, ed. Colleen J. Sheehy and Thomas Swiss (Minneapolis: University of Minnesota Press, 2009), 213–24.

INDEX

FREDDY CRISTÓBAL DOMÍNGUEZ was born in Brooklyn, New York, and was educated at Brown University and Princeton University. He is author of *Radicals in Exile: English Books During the Reign of Philip II* and coeditor of *Political and Religious Practice in the Early Modern British World*. He is currently associate professor of history at the University of Arkansas and lives in Fayetteville with his wife and four children.